JOHN,
Your Name
Is Famous

JOHN,
Your Name
Is Famous

*Highlights,
Anecdotes &
Trivia about the
Name John and
the People Who
Made It Great*

*By Alvin, Virginia, Robert, Linda,
Laura and Kevin SILVERSTEIN*

AVSTAR Publishing Corp.
P.O. Box 537
Lebanon, NJ 08833

JOHN,
Your Name
Is Famous

Highlights,
Anecdotes &
Trivia about the
Name John and
the People Who
Made It Great

By the **SILVERSTEINS**

Copyright ©1989 AVSTAR Publishing Corp.
P.O. Box 537, Lebanon, NJ 08833

All rights reserved. No part of this book may be reproduced or trans-
mitted in any form or by any means, electronic or mechanical, without
written permission from the publisher.

The authors and publisher have carefully researched numerous sources
to ensure the accuracy and completeness of the information in this book,
but we assume no responsibility for any errors or omissions. Any
apparent slights against people or organizations mentioned in *JOHN,
Your Name Is Famous*, are unintentional.

Manufactured in the United States of America

Library of Congress Catalog Card No. 89-85204

Library of Congress Cataloging-in-Publication Date

John, your name is famous: highlights, anecdotes & trivia about the name John and the people who
    made it great/by Alvin, Virginia, Robert, Linda, Laura, and Kevin Silverstein.
        p.   cm.
    Includes bibliographical references.
    ISBN 0-9623653-0-0
    1. John (Name) — Miscellanea. I. Silverstein, Alvin.
CS2391, J6J64 1989   89-85204
929.4'4—dc20   CIP

Acknowledgments

The authors are grateful to all those who kindly supplied photographs and information for use in this book. Special thanks go to the staff of the New York Public Library and the Hunterdon County Library, for their help and resourcefulness.

In sifting through the huge volumes of information, we were immensely aided by the members of our research and office staff. For their conscientious work and creative suggestions we want to thank Nancy Broadwell, Isabelle Brown, Angela Cannon, Linda Carberry, Gloria Green, Lisa Gumul, Dolores Hooper, Scott Ramsay, and Nicole Vignec.

Thanks, too, to our typographer, TeleSet, for their capable work and helpful suggestions.

Picture Credits

NYPL = New York Public Library Picture Collection

p.3 NYPL; p.6 Deere & Company; p.10 Bettman Archive; p. 13 NYPL; p. 17 Library of Congress; p.23 NASA; p. 28 Mrs. Emundo Lasalle, New York; p. 34 IBM; p.37 Edward Steichen, Museum of Modern Art; p. 41 CBS Radio; p. 44 John Houseman; pp. 47, 50, 52, 54 NYPL; p.59 J.H.W. Fischbein, Stadelsches Kunstinstitut, Frankfurt; p. 61 NYPL; p.63 engraving by J. Posselwhite; p. 66 Gale Research International Portrait Gallery; p.69 photo: Rex Rystedt, Performing Artservices, Inc.; p.70 RCA Records; p.72 Mozart Museum, Salzburg; p.76 Library of Congress; p.78 Vatican; p.83 NYPL; p.84 engraving by F. Mackenzie; p.86 photo: George R. King; p.91 Warner Bros.; p.92 Spectrum Sports; p.93 Jack Nicklaus Marketing Services; p.96 NYPL; p.99 Library of Congress; p.103 engraving by I.B. Forrest from painting by J.B. Copley; p.109 American Museum of Natural History; p.110 engraving by George Perine; p.115 Gale Research Internation Portrait Gallery; p.117 NYPL; p.120 Herald Tribune; p.124 Associated Press; p. 171 (1) PolyGram Records, House of Cash; p.171 (2) John Glenn; p.171 (3) photo: Douglas Edmunds, Colbert Artists Management Inc.; p.171 (4) Hanson & Schwam, public relations; p.171 (5) Citizens for Jack Kemp.

For John

Name: _____

Birthdate: _____

Hometown: _____

Nickname: _____

Background: _____

_____

_____

Highlights and achievements: _____

_____

_____

_____

_____

_____

_____

CONTENTS

CHAPTER 1

JOHN IS A FAMOUS NAME

The JOHN Clan

Many people named John have reached the top: presidents, entertainers, sports stars, military heroes. In every field, in every area of life, Johns are achievers.

The Johns of the past and present can be thought of as a clan, sharing something important: an old and famous first name. For centuries, John has been the most common name in all the English-speaking countries.

The Many Names of JOHN

The John clan is a surprisingly large one. There are more than 100 variations of the name John in over thirty different languages around the world. These variations include: **Evan, Giovanni, Hans, Ian, Ivan, Jack, Jan, Jean, Jock, Johannes, Jon, Jonas, Jonathan, Juan, Owen, Sean, and Zane.**

The Meaning of JOHN

John comes from the Hebrew *Johanan* (pronounced "Yo-HAHN-ahn"), which means "God-is-gracious." It is found in the Old Testament and was a common Jewish name.

1

JOHN Through the Ages

Johanan passed into the Greek language as *Joannes* (or Iaoness), and into Latin as *Johannes* (again the J is pronounced as "Y"). Two important saints were named John — John the Baptist and John the Apostle. (Actually, their names were Johanan.) Wherever Christianity spread, this important Christian name spread with it as believers named their children after the saints.

English JOHN Beginnings

John was not a common English name until the eleventh century. The Norman conquerors brought it to Britain in various forms like the old French *Jehan*. Jehan became anglicized and was shortened to *John*. At one time in the 1500s, from one quarter to one third of all boys born in England were named John.

The Name JOHN, Today

John continued to be a popular name over the years, and a study in the 1950s concluded there were about six million people named John in the United States alone. Today there are about eight million Johns in the U.S. — not even counting such variations as Jack, Jon, Sean, Juan, and dozens of others.

The "JOHN, Your Name Is Famous" Book

In the pages that follow, we'll get a glimpse of the enormous impact the Johns of the past have had on our modern world. We can look forward to a better, safer, more comfortable life in the future because of the contributions of members of the John clan who are alive and productive today. Johns of every age have left their mark and added to the pride of those who share their name.

2

FAMOUS JOHN FIRSTS

John Quincy Adams

A Most Unusual Press Conference

President **John Quincy Adams** was having a private swim in the Potomac back in 1829. As it turned out, it wasn't very private. A female journalist grabbed his clothes, which he had left

3

on the bank, and refused to return them unless he granted her an interview. He did; it was the first Presidential press conference.

Nonstop Over the Atlantic

The *London Daily Mail* was offering 10,000 pounds to the first one to cross the Atlantic Ocean, nonstop, in an airplane. World War I had ended, and aviation was in its heyday. Hardly a month went by without some kind of new air record being set. Dozens of aviation teams got ready for the new competition. The flight would be nearly 2,000 miles, and no one had come close to such a feat before. But a British team, Captain **John W. Alcock** and his navigator, Arthur W. Brown, made the trip successfully in sixteen hours and twelve minutes, starting out on June 14, 1919 and landing the next day in a marshy bog near Clifton, Ireland. They were hailed as heroes in England. The two pioneers were knighted and, of course, received the 10,000 pounds.

Birth of the Boob Tube

For most people today, life without television would be hard to imagine. And yet a generation or so ago, TV was just beginning to get off the ground. Many people contributed to its development, but **John Logie Baird** was the first one to produce television pictures of objects in motion, in 1924. Four years later, he successfully demonstrated color television and was able to transmit TV images across the Atlantic Ocean.

Up, Up and Away

There's something about the sight of brightly colored balloons up in the sky that brings on a rush of excitement. Balloon festivals draw people from far and wide. Some come to watch, but others gather the courage to fulfill a fantasy and fly high above it all. George Washington watched while **Jean-Pierre-François**

Blanchard made the first balloon flight in America, back in 1793. Blanchard was the number one balloonist of his time. He and **Dr. John Jeffries** were the first to cross the English Channel in a balloon (in 1785). They barely made it, managing to stay aloft by throwing all their cargo overboard — except for one package, the first international airmail, which they delivered safely in France. Blanchard also made the first balloon flights in England, Belgium, North America, and Poland.

XTRA, XTRA Read All About It

For many people the day wouldn't be complete without reading the newspaper. All across the world, practically every substantial town has its own paper. The first successful newspaper in the American colonies, the *Boston News-Letter*, was started in 1704 by a postmaster named **John Campbell**. When the Revolutionary War came along, a new nation was born. But alas, America's first newspaper was discontinued.

Blowing Bubbles

Did you ever notice that most major league baseball players chew? Whether it be chewing gum or tobacco, they seem to have their jaws constantly moving. And of course, the major leaguers are the *best*. Could there be something to this? Experiments have demonstrated that chewing sends extra blood to the brain and increases brain wave activity. If ever you are nodding off to sleep, try chewing gum. It'll wake you up!

The first chewing gum ever manufactured was produced by **John B. Curtis** in Bangor, Maine, in 1848. Such exotic flavors as "Sugar Cream," "200 Lump Spruce," and "Licorice Lulu" were offered to the public. Curtis later introduced the gum to the western territories — the first traveling salesman to represent an Eastern firm there.

5

John Deere

The Singing Plow

The rich farmlands of the Midwest might never have become America's breadbasket if it were not for an enterprising blacksmith named **John Deere**. Nobody could make a plow that could cut through the thick, gummy soil until 1837, when Deere took an old circular saw that a sawmill had thrown away and turned it into the first steel plow. The plow vibrated with a singing sound. Soon Deere had a thriving company producing his singing plows. Today John Deere is a world leader in gasoline tractors. The first one was manufactured by **John Froelich** in 1892. His company was bought by the John Deere company around the turn of the century, and now, with the sixth generation of Deeres at the helm, the company is still a giant in U.S. industry.

6

Mmm Mmm Good ...

When Andy Warhol painted a can of Campbell Soup, there was instant recognition on the part of the viewer, and for some strange reason a "masterpiece" was born. Campbell soup has almost become the generic name for canned, condensed soup in this country.

The first canned soup was invented by Dr. **John T. Dorrance** in 1899. The soup was produced by the Joseph Campbell Preserve Company, which became the Campbell Soup Company in 1915.

Batter Up!

It was the ninth inning, and the Cleveland Spiders were trailing the Brooklyn Ward's Wonders. The manager of the Spiders sent their backup catcher, **John J. Doyle,** to the plate. With a runner on first, Doyle smashed a single to advance the runner to third. This was Doyle's first pinch hit in his career. In fact, it was the first pinch hit *ever* in professional baseball. It happened on June 7, 1892.

Help Your Son and Make a Fortune

Helping his ten-year-old son changed **Dr. John B. Dunlop's** life. The boy was having trouble riding his tricycle on the bumpy roads in the Scottish countryside. So Dunlop got the idea of putting an air-filled rubber tube inside the tires of the tricycle. Thus was born the pneumatic tire (tyre in British), which became the basis of all modern tires that propel today's trucks and cars. Dunlop, the country veterinary surgeon who came up with the idea, became an entrepreneur and went on to earn a fortune.

The Modern Elixir

Reading the label on a box of Arm & Hammer Baking Soda is a mind-boggling experience. This substance, the manufacturer insists, is good for baking cakes and cookies, absorbing odors from rugs and refrigerators, neutralizing excess stomach acid, treating minor skin irritations, insect bites, sun and wind burn, prickly heat, and more. Baking soda (sodium bicarbonate) was first commercially produced in 1846 by **John Dwight** and his partner, Dr. Austin Church.

Fitch, Not Fulton

Most school children are taught that Robert Fulton developed the first successful steamboat in America. But the credit really belongs to **John Fitch**. A surveyor and Revolutionary War veteran, he successfully demonstrated his forty-five-foot steamboat on August 22, 1787. He then built a larger boat, which carried passengers and freight from Philadelphia to Burlington. He received a patent for steamboats on August 26, 1791. A storm destroyed his next steamboat — and his career. He died poor and unheralded. Although Robert Fulton did not launch a steamboat until 1798, long after Fitch died, he nonetheless received worldwide recognition for the invention.

Across Niagara Falls on a Rope

Jean-Pierre-François Gravelet was a tightrope walker, but more than anything — he was a showman. On June 30, 1859, before an excited crowd of 5000, he made the first crossing of Niagara Falls on a tightrope suspended more than 150 feet above the raging water. While the crowd held their breath, he repeated the stunt, each time with a new theatrical twist: wearing a blindfold, bound in a sack, pushing a wheelbarrow, walking on stilts, carrying a man on his back, and even making and eating an omelette on the way!

Father of the Plastics Industry

It is difficult to imagine a world without plastics. Tools, furniture, toys, even automobile parts are made from them. They're an integral part of our throwaway society. The discovery that opened up the plastics industry was celluloid, first patented in 1869. Its inventor, **John W. Hyatt,** received $10,000 in reward money from a billiard ball manufacturer for its first application. Other applications, from wrapping paper to motion picture film and beyond, transformed our society. It was the beginning of the plastics revolution, which is still in full swing and continues to make our lives more comfortable, safer, and more exciting.

Beleaguered Champion

In 1908 **Jack Johnson** became the first black boxer ever to win a world championship. After his victory a frantic search ensued for a "great white hope" to reclaim the title. One fight against a former champion resulted in racial violence across the country. In 1912 Johnson was convicted of violating the Mann Act by crossing a state border with his white fiancee. He fled to Canada while he was out on bail and spent the next seven years as a fugitive. After defending the title successfully several times in Paris, Johnson finally lost to Jess Willard in Havana, Cuba in 1915. He later claimed that he was paid to let Willard win, but others have suggested that he did it in hopes of avoiding his jail sentence. If so, the ploy didn't work; he eventually gave himself up and served his sentence in Leavenworth. Johnson's career was captured in a play, and later a movie, titled "The Great White Hope," both starring James Earl Jones.

JFK: Helper of the Needy

While Campaigning for the Presidency of the United States, **John F. Kennedy** toured the poverty-stricken areas of West Virginia. He was so overwhelmed by the deprivation he saw that he vowed if ever he were elected president, he would help these people, and all those like them across the nation. He was elected, and in 1961 the nation's first food stamp program was started. This program has helped millions of needy Americans over difficult times. Most have gone on to lead productive lives.

9

Jack Johnson

The Vice President Took His Job Away

Today the Vice President serves as the president pro tem of the United States Senate. He presides over the daily sessions and casts a ballot in case of a tie vote. But before the election of the first Vice President, this role was filled by **John Langdon**, a senator from New Hampshire. Langdon counted the votes of the Electoral College and established that George Washington was to be the first President of the United States, and John Adams the first Vice President. On April 21, 1789 when Adams became Vice President, Langdon lost his job.

Some years later, Langdon turned down a chance to win the job back. The Republican Party caucus of 1812 voted to nominate him as Vice President, the running mate of presidential candidate James Madison. But Langdon declined the nomination.

I Now Pronounce You Man and Wife

Millions of marriages take place in the United States every year. Each day, thousands of Americans tie the knot. So what's the big deal about the marriage of **John Laydon** and Ann Burrows? They were the first couple to be married in the American colonies. The wedding took place in Virginia, in 1609.

No Nicks, No Cuts

Rare is the man or woman who has used a razor without ever having been nicked. And yet today we use *safety* razors. Imagine the amount of blood flowing if unprotected razors were used. Well, for centuries that is precisely what was used. But in 1762, a professional barber, **Jean Jacques Perret**, invented a razor protected by a metal guard. This effectively prevented bad nicks. The Perret razor was rather heavy and somewhat awkward to use. The modern T-shaped razor was developed in the United States in the 1880s. The original models required constant sharpening. Today, with our throwaway society, we just reach for a new blade — or even a new razor.

11

A Good Read

Can you imagine waiting in a doctor's office with no magazines to read? People love magazines, and you can find one on almost any subject. In 1633, German theological poet **Johann Rist** published the first edition of his *Edifying Monthly Discussions*. It certainly didn't have the circulation of *Time* or *Newsweek*, and it only lasted for five years, but this magazine of poetry and theology was the very first magazine ever.

Suspended in Air

There is something precarious about a suspension bridge. Even though engineers' calculations clearly demonstrate that the bridge will hold up under the severest of hurricanes, the average person can't help but worry about these swaying structures. Suspension bridges did not reach their full potential until the introduction of wire cables capable of bearing enormous loads. The first wire cable suspension bridge was completed in 1845 under the supervision of German immigrant, **John A. Roebling**. Roebling went on to build a railway suspension bridge over Niagara Falls in 1854. But his crowning achievement was the construction of the Brooklyn Bridge, which was completed in 1883, long after his death in 1869.

A Black Blazing New Trails

John B. Russwurm's life was filled with firsts. He was the first black to graduate from a U.S. college: Bowdoin College in 1826. The next year he was the first black to edit a newspaper: *Freedom's Journal*. This landmark paper was a four-page weekly published in New York City, which espoused the cause of the anti-slavery movement. But Russwurm soon became frustrated with his efforts, believing the blacks would never be freed. He left the U.S. in 1829 to settle in Liberia, where he served as the governor of a colony.

How Do I Get There From Here?

Do you remember when road maps were free for the asking at any gas station? That perk of modern living went the way of the dinosaurs after the oil crisis in the seventies. Now, if you want a map you have to pay for it. Many drivers do, and keep a well-thumbed map in the glove compartment. Back in the horse and buggy days, maps were just as useful for people who wanted to know how to get from one place to another. The first person to devise a road map for public use was **John Tulley**, in 1698. Although no cars existed then, *Tulley's Almanac* provided the traveler with a handy list of towns and the roads connecting them.

John Tyler

13

First White House Wedding

John Tyler was the first Vice President ever to reach the nation's highest office because of the death of the President. Tyler was a maverick, alienating his own Democratic Party and the opposition Whigs, as well. So when William Henry Harrison died in 1841, Tyler was almost made "acting president" with limited powers. But he fought off these attempts and was sworn in as America's tenth president. President Tyler's wife, Letitia Christian Polk, died in the White House in 1842, after nearly thirty years of marriage. Tyler married Julia Gardiner, the daughter of a New York Senator, in 1844, becoming the first president to marry while in office.

Double No-Hit Vander Meer

Baseball records are made to be broken. But one record will probably never be topped. The odds against pitching a no-hitter are extraordinary. In addition to outstanding skill, an unusual amount of luck is involved. Anything can happen in a baseball game. A batter can be completely fooled by a pitch, hit the ball off the end of the bat, and it drops in for a bloop hit. **Johnny Vander Meer** pitched not one, but two no-hitters — *back to back!* While pitching for Cincinnati at old Crosley Field during the 1938 season, he blanked the Boston Braves, 3-0. Four days later, against the backdrop of a hostile crowd, he shut out the Brooklyn Dodgers, 6-0. For eighteen straight innings, he allowed not a single hit!

Gotta Match, Buddy?

Even though we have self-starting gas stoves and electric stoves, cigarette lighters, and many more modern conveniences, the old-fashioned match is still useful. The match was actually invented by accident. One day in 1826, British chemist **John Walker** was attempting to develop a new explosive. He had mixed antimony sulfide, potassium chlorate, gum, and starch. Using a sliver of wood, he stirred the messy-looking concoction, then removed the stick and laid it aside. Later, when he was about to reuse the stirrer, Walker noticed that a small, teardrop-shaped bit of the solution had dried onto the end of it. He flicked the stick against the stone floor of the laboratory to scrape away the annoying residue. Suddenly there was a flash of light, and the piece of wood caught fire. The match had been invented!

Boston's First Citizen

Boston has a rich history and a fabulous heritage. It was one of the first major cities established in this country. The man most responsible for its founding was **John Winthrop**. Appointed the governor of the Massachusetts Bay Colony in 1629, he sailed off to the New World the following year, with five ships carrying about 900 settlers. September 17, 1630 is the historic day when Boston began its existence. It quickly developed into an important center of commerce and culture in the early colonial days. Winthrop, meanwhile, was elected governor of Massachusetts in 1631 — the first officially accredited election in America.

The First Gun-Totin' Showdown

The Virginian (1902) is a classic that has been read by millions. It's story about a cowboy — the first cowboy story ever written. It contains the first "showdown" ever to appear in fiction, with the hero standing up against the "bad guy." The author, **Owen Wister**, was a Philadelphia lawyer who spent his summers out West and eventually turned his hobby into a full-time writing career. He went on to write a number of other works, but none matched the acclaim achieved by the *The Virginian*.

15

CHAPTER 3

NICKNAMES AND ALIASES

Doctor My-Book

John Abernathy (1764-1831)

    John Abernathy was a very successful English surgeon who wrote a book entitled *Surgical Observations*. He took every opportunity, to the point of being annoying at times, to recommend his book — even to those who would hardly understand its contents. Soon everyone was calling him *Doctor My-Book*.

The Colossus of Independence

John Adams (1735-1826)

    John Adams, our second President, was clearly a fat man —so much so that some called him as *His Rotundity*. But others spoke more kindly of him. Thomas Jefferson, the author of the Declaration of Independence, referred to Adams as *The Colossus of Independence* in recognition of this American patriot's critical role in pushing for freedom from Britain during the meetings of the Continental Congress.

The Great Profile

John Barrymore (1882-1942)

    One of the greatest romantic film stars, **John Barrymore** was known as *The Great Profile*. He had more than his good looks,

John Barrymore

though. For years he continued to turn in masterful performances on screen, while in his private life he was battling a chronic drinking problem and four failed marriages. Larger than life, Barrymore was himself the subject of a film, *Good Night, Sweet Prince*, in 1944.

The World's Greatest Lover

Giovanni Jacopo Casanova (1725-1798)

He was *The World's Greatest Lover* — or so he said, in his memoirs. Even today the world believes his claims, for his name is a

17

synonym for a man who charms and seduces members of the opposite sex. In his lifetime, thousands of women succumbed to **Casanova's** charms. This great lover led quite a varied and exciting life. He was a violinist, businessman, alchemist, diplomat, librarian, journalist, spy, and wheeler-dealer extraordinaire. Reflecting on his adventures in his last years, Casanova told his life story with such vivid detail and wit that his memoirs are still read, two centuries after his death.

Johnny Shiloh

John Lincoln Clem (1851-1937)

Young **John Lincoln Clem** was the inspiration for the patriotic song, *The Drummer Boy of Shiloh*. He tried to join the Union Army at the age of nine during the Civil War but was turned down, so he just joined — unofficially. He picked out the 22nd Michigan Infantry and served as a drummer. The officers of the troop donated his pay of $13 a month. In 1862, at the Battle of Shiloh, an artillery shell smashed his drum to pieces as he was beating it. Miraculously, Johnny was unharmed. News of this incident spread like wildfire throughout the Union Army. Johnny of Shiloh became an instant hero.

The Youngest Millionaire

Jackie Coogan (1914-1984)

Although **Jackie Coogan** earned millions of dollars as a child actor, he never got to spend much more than a tiny fraction of this sum. Jackie's movie career began when he was barely eighteen months old. At the age of four he was appearing regularly in an Annette Kellerman revue. Charlie Chaplin happened to see him acting in the show in Los Angeles, and he cast the child as his costar in the feature-length movie *The Kid* in 1921. The movie was a hit and Coogan became a superstar earning over $4 million. The press called him *The Youngest Millionaire*. But when Jackie came of age and tried to collect the money, a lengthy court battle ensued after which the star received only a little more than $100,000 — his parents had spent the rest!

The Second-Worst Poet

Sir John Denham (1615-1669)

    John Denham was one of the most innovative and popular English poets of the late seventeenth and early eighteenth centuries. During the Civil War in England he staunchly supported Charles II. His efforts were richly rewarded after the Restoration — he was made a knight of the Bath, elected to the Royal Society, and served as a member of Parliament.

    When George Withers, the Puritan poet, was arrested and sentenced to death for treason, Denham approached the King with the argument: "If your Majesty kills Withers, I will then be the worst poet in England." The King spared Withers, and thereafter, John Denham was known as *The Second-Worst Poet.*

The Best Abused Man in England

John Dennis (1657-1734)

    When you attack renowned and influential people, be prepared for the worst. English critic and dramatist, **John Dennis**, learned this lesson the hard way. Dennis insisted that passion was the most important element in poetry. He was not a very successful dramatist, but he passionately expressed his views in his essays criticizing many other writers of his day. One of them was the famous poet Alexander Pope, whom he called "a hunchback'd toad" whose deformed body mirrored a deformed mind. Pope retaliated in kind, and others like master satirist Jonathan Swift joined in. Dennis was attacked so much and by so many people that he became known as *The Best Abused Man in England.*

Sean Aloysius O'Feeney

John Ford (1895-1973)

    Director **John Ford** did more than any other man in Hollywood to popularize the Western. In a career spanning sixty years, he directed 136 features, including such classics as *Stagecoach* and *She Wore A Yellow Ribbon*. He virtually created John Wayne, who called him "Coach" and regarded his mentor as both friend and role model. After they watched the rushes of *Stagecoach*, Wayne told Ford, "Well, you know... I'm just playin' you."

Gruff, tough, the epitome of the Western hero, Ford was actually an Easterner, born in Maine. The thirteenth child of Irish immigrants, he was originally named *Sean Aloysius O'Feeney*.

John Elroy Sanford

Redd Foxx (1922-)

Redd Foxx made a name for himself as the King of Adult Humor. Over ten million copies of his comedy albums have been sold over the years. He made an even bigger impression as the crusty but lovable old junk man, Fred Sanford, on the TV series, *Sanford & Son*. The show first came out in 1972, but it can still be seen today in reruns across the country. The name of the lead character was actually Foxx's own: He was born *John Elroy Sanford*. He took his stage name from a combination of an early nickname, Chicago Red ("Red" is a slang term for a light-skinned black), and the famous baseball player, Jimmy Foxx, with the sly red fox of children's stories and the term "foxy" in mind, too.

The Pathfinder

John Charles Fremont (1813-1890)

John Fremont's life was strewn with failure. He was the first Presidential candidate of the new Republican Party in the 1856 election, but he didn't win. He was fired from his Civil War job as head of the Western Department when he ordered the confiscation of many rebel properties. He lost a fortune trying to build a railroad to the Pacific in 1870.

Before these misadventures, Fremont had earned an impressive reputation as an explorer and guide as he led four expeditions over the Rocky Mountains to California and mapped out the Oregon Trail. For these daring exploits he earned the sobriquet, *The Pathfinder.*

Bet-a-Million

John Warne Gates (1855-1911)

Anyone who could parlay $8,000 into $90,000,000 in twenty years must be quite a good businessman. And yet other men of the business world were wary of getting involved with **John Gates**. He was a risk taker — a real gambler. His speculations in the stock market were so daring that he quickly earned the sobriquet *Bet-a-Million-Gates.* Gates would bet on almost anything. Once, he bet young John Drake (whose family founded Drake University) $11,000, that more flies would be attracted to his cup of coffee than to Drake's cup. Of course Gates won. What Drake didn't know was that Gates had spiked his own coffee with six spoonfuls of sugar.

The Yankee Doodle Dandy

John Hancock (1737-1793)

Just before the outbreak of the Revolutionary War, **John Hancock** was the richest merchant in Boston. He was not shy about living in the grand style. His servants all carried arms, much in the manner of a king's guard. Because he obviously sympathized with the rebellious colonists, the British sneeringly referred to him as *King Hancock.* Others, going further, called him *King of the Smugglers*, which happened to have more than a grain of truth in it. But the people of Boston considered Hancock their hero and called him *The Yankee Doodle Dandy.*

Moneybag

Ivan I (1304?-1340)

Most rulers conquer new land by force. But when you're rich, why not try money — why not buy it? That is precisely what

Ivan I, grand prince of Moscow, did. He gained his wealth through thrift and financial shrewdness, and more than earned the nickname *Moneybag*. By forming alliances with neighboring rulers, he expanded the influence of Moscow, making it the most powerful and richest principality in northeastern Russia.

The Gay Young Bachelor

John F. Kennedy (1917-1963)

Before he was married, **John F. Kennedy** was quite a ladies' man and was involved in several near-scandals. While in congress, he was called *The Gay Young Bachelor*. After he died, the media taboo on his sex life was lifted, and many women came forward claiming to have had affairs with Kennedy — not all of them before he married. Kennedy is said to have been romantically involved with Jayne Mansfield, Judith Exner, Gene Tierney, and Marilyn Monroe.

The Paper King

John Law (1671-1729)

In the early 18th century gold and silver were the only means of settling a financial transaction. **John Law** proposed a scheme for substituting paper money for coins. His countrymen in Scotland turned him down, but the French were strapped for cash as a result of the extensive wars of Louis XIV. They invited Law to France to set his plan in motion. For a while it worked. Law founded a bank with authority to issue paper money and made a fortune, gaining the nickname of *The Paper King*. But Law floated too much stock on risky land developments, and the bubble burst. Panicky investors demanded gold for their paper money, and the bank failed. Law was forced to flee, without a franc.

The Elephant Man

John Merrick (1862-1890)

At birth, **John Merrick** seemed normal. But when he was

five, a series of strange changes took place. His head grew to a monstrous size, three feet in circumference. Flaps of skin hung loosely from his head and face, hiding his expressions. He lost almost all control of his voice. His right arm and leg were grotesque. To some people he looked more like an elephant than a man. And so the world called him *The Elephant Man*. A century after his death, the story of the tormented Elephant Man gained new familiarity through a popular play and a movie about his life. Recently he was the center of attention again when superstar Michael Jackson tried to purchase his remains.

John A. Powers

23

The Voice of the Astronauts

John A Powers (1922-1980)

"This is Mission Control. Everything is A-OK" When this message rang out to America, everyone knew who was talking. It was **John "Shorty" Powers**, *The Voice of the Astronauts*. During the 1960s when America was fulfilling the dream launched by President Kennedy — to land a man on the Moon before 1970 — the voice informing the public of the progress of the program was as well known as any in the nation. Powers coined the phrase "A-OK," which for a while was as familiar as "How are you?" After the Moon landing, his voice faded into history.

The Man with the Golden Flute

Jean-Pierre Rampal (1922-)

Jean-Pierre Rampal's handcrafted 14 karat solid gold flute, gleaming on the concert stage during his virtuoso performances, has won him the sobriquet, *The Man with the Golden Flute*. He dislikes the nickname and claims it was mere happenstance that he grew fond of a wonderful gold flute that he found early in his career. Since then he has tried flutes made of other metals but didn't like them. A platinum flute, he says, had too cold a sound; the tone of the gold one is warmer.

Probably the most recorded classical musician in history, Rampal originally intended to become a doctor. He dropped out of medical school to join the Resistance when the Germans occupied France; after the war he chose a musical career instead of returning to medicine.

The Prince of Satirists

Hans Sachs (1494-1576)

Hans Sachs started off his career as a cobbler, but he became one of the most prolific literary figures who ever lived. Altogether he composed more than 6,300 pieces: more than 4,000 songs, 2,000 tales in verse, and 208 plays. He was the real-life

24

inspiration for the hero of Richard Wagner's great opera, *Die Meistersinger von Nurnberg*. But he was also a pesky critic of the status quo, finding fault with the nobility, clergy, and just about every aspect of a society that treated the common folk harshly. For this he was dubbed *The Prince of Satirists*.

The Wizard

John III Sobieski *(1629-1696)*

John III Sobieski was so brilliant on the battlefield that his enemies, the Tatars, were convinced he had supernatural powers. So he became known as *The Wizard*. The admiration of his people for his smashing victories over the Ottoman Turks and other foes brought him to the throne of Poland in 1674. Unfortunately, his wizardry didn't extend to domestic matters, and his troublesome family and subjects made his last years miserable. While Sobieski lived, Poland achieved greatness, but after his death, the incessant squabbles of his countrymen ultimately led to the dismemberment of this once great nation.

Snowshoe Thompson

John A. Thompson *(1827-1876)*

The mail must go through! That was easier said than done a century ago. Intrepid settlers in their wagon trains made the trek to California, but then it was often difficult to keep in touch with the folks back east — especially when heavy winter snows made the mountain passes impassable. For twenty years, from 1856 until 1876, Norwegian immigrant **John A. Thompson** was the dependable mailman who linked miners in isolated camps with the rest of the country. Working out of the Sacramento post office, he made the ninety-mile California-to-Nevada mail run with his trusty skis. Not even twenty-five-foot snowdrifts could keep mailman *Snowshoe Thompson* from his appointed rounds. For thirteen years, until the Central Pacific Railroad was completed, Thompson provided the only mail link between California and the rest of the nation.

The Duke

John Wayne (1907-1979)

John Wayne is a Hollywood legend. Born Marion Morrison, he took a stage name that sounded more fitting for the strong, silent, courageous American hero he played in his films. Friends knew him as *The Duke*. Oddly, that nickname came from a dog he had owned when he was young. Duke was an Airedale terrier. He and Wayne were inseparable. Jokingly, the firemen at the local station called Wayne by his dog's name — Duke — and it stuck.

The Most Popular DJ In The World

Wolfman Jack (Robert Smith) (1939-)

Wolfman Jack is the best known DJ in the world. His raspy voice first hit the airwaves in the late 1950s down in Mexico, then moved up to Los Angeles. By the mid-1970s he was an international success, with a syndicated radio show broadcast around the world and a TV music show that ran for eight years. Born *Robert Smith*, he loved listening to music on the radio, especially when the platters were spun by his favorite DJ, Dr. Jive, whose line was, "What's up, Jack?" Later, working as a DJ in Mexico, he used the name "Big Smith with the Records." But then a fan sent him a cartoon of a wolf, and he changed his name legally to Wolfman Jack. The howling DJ has been the subject of several songs, written by artists like the Guess Who, Freddie King, Leon Russell, and Todd Rundgren.

The Morning Star of the Reformation

John Wycliffe (1330?-1384)

The Black Plague, the Hundred Years War, constant power struggles between church and state, and the sufferings of the common people made fourteenth-century Europe ripe for revolution. **John Wycliffe**, an English theologian, sowed the seeds for change by declaring that unjust political or religious rulers could not claim that God's will required men to obey them. Wycliffe's

26

followers, the Lollards, translated the Bible into English, making God's word accessible to the common man and undercutting the church's monopoly on religious teachings. Wycliffe's ideas lived on, greatly influencing religious and secular thought in the centuries that followed. He was a true forerunner of reform — *The Morning Star of the Reformation.*

———————

CHAPTER 4

JOHN IN THE ART WORLD

John James Audubon

The Bird Lover

John James Audubon *(1785-1851)*
— *American artist and naturalist* —

    John James Audubon was such a spoiled child, no one thought he would ever amount to anything. He wasn't very good at school, and he was even worse at the business ventures his rich father set up for him. But Audubon loved to draw, and he loved nature. His great work, *Birds of America*, brought to the public more than 1000 life-size drawings of over 500 different species of birds. Many of the birds he captured on paper are now extinct, and his drawings are our only memory of their existence.

"The Best Painter of Them All"

Giovanni Bellini (c1430-1516)
— Italian Renaissance painter —

Giovanni Bellini was one of the first of the great Venetian painters. It was largely his influence and that of his students — Titian, for example — that helped make Venice one of the world's greatest art centers. Bellini was the chief painter of the Republic of Venice for the last thirty-three years of his life. His art school became extremely popular, and his influence in innovative ideas and techniques spread throughout the art world. While visiting Venice in 1506, world renowned artist Albrecht Durer wrote that Bellini "is very old, and still he is the best painter of them all."

Sculptor and Architect for Popes

Gian Lorenzo Bernini (1598-1680)
— Italian sculptor, architect, playwright —

In the days of the Italian Renaissance, the highest goal for a sculptor was to work for the Pope. **Gian Bernini** worked for *eight* popes. He was so famous in his time that when he traveled to Paris in 1665, crowds lined the streets of every city he passed through, just to get a glimpse of him. He created the Baroque style of sculpture and thus influenced this art form for centuries after his death.

Greener than Grass

John Constable (1776-1837)
— British landscape painter —

Anyone can see beauty in a country scene. But putting that

29

scene on canvas in a way that makes others share the beauty is a skill that few possess. **John Constable** could capture qualities in a scene from nature that made the canvas spring to life. His rich colors set a new style — so much so that some of the great artists of the time, including Eugene Delacroix, adopted some of his techniques. To this day, Constable remains one of the great landscape painters of all time.

The Best Colonial Artist

John Singleton Copley (1738-1815)
— Colonial American portrait and historical painter —
   Sometimes practice doesn't make perfect. Colonial artist **John Singleton Copley** had a tremendous reputation as a portrait painter in Boston. Even today he is considered one of the best of that period. His reputation brought him to England, where he painted with and learned from some of Europe's greatest artists. His style became more polished and refined, but that powerful freshness and charm disappeared from his works, and he became just another artist.

The Man Who Loved to Paint

Jean-Baptiste-Camille Corot (1795-1875)
— French landscape and portrait painter —
   Jean-Baptiste-Camille Corot never married. The only thing that really interested him was painting. His last words were, "With all my heart I hope there is painting in Heaven." He was quite popular during his lifetime and left behind three thousand paintings. Corot was a polished and professional painter, but his most memorable works are his rough "sketch" paintings that he did directly from nature. For the first time unpolished paintings became accepted as works of art, and the stage was set for the Impressionists to capture the hearts of the world.

The Wizard of Cartoons

Johnny Hart (1931-)
— American cartoonist —

Cartoonist **Johnny Hart** has been taking us back in time to funnier worlds for over thirty years, with his cartoon strips *B.C.* and the *Wizard of Id*. Hart makes us laugh at ourselves and our world with his stone-age B.C. as his characters discover the wheel and life's funnier moments, and he lives out his own ruling fantasies in the zany mythical world of the pint-sized King and his Wizard of Id. Our days just wouldn't be the same without these comics.

Royal Design

Hans Holbein, the Younger (1497-1543)
— German painter, designer and draftsman —

Hans, Holbein, the Younger painted portraits so well that King Henry VIII sent him out to travel the realm, painting likenesses of prospective brides. With a total of six wives, he kept Holbein busy. The artist also designed all the King's robes, as well as weaponry, jewelry, and whatever else took Henry's fancy. The talented painter's life was cut short by the plague during an epidemic in 1543.

Lost Touch with Reality

John Everett Millais (1829-1896)
— British painter and illustrator —

Some people criticize Normal Rockwell's paintings as too lifelike, almost "photographic." More than a century ago, **John Millais** received the same criticism for his paintings. In time the public began to appreciate them, and he became a celebrity. But with fame and popularity, the rebel turned respectable. His style changed, and though he stayed popular, his impact on art diminished as his originality ebbed.

Jack the Dripper

Jackson Pollock (1912-1956)
— American painter —

Artists always use paint brushes, don't they? Not **Jackson Pollock**, who made a name for himself by dripping paint onto his canvases. His goal was to let his subconscious mind create whatever it pleased. Likewise, the viewers of his works should leave themselves completely open as well. At one point he numbered all his paintings, rather than title them, so that people wouldn't be influenced in their interpretations. He was so intent on letting his paintings having a life of their own, that he would "drip" over anything with an identifiable form.

Innovative Architecture on a Grand Scale

John Calvin Portman, Jr. (1924-)
— American architect, developer —

It would be hard to drive through Atlanta, Georgia for very long without passing a building that **John Portman** played a role in designing and building. The famous Peachtree Center was entirely his work. When he completed Atlanta's Hyatt Regency Hotel, with its huge atrium lobby, over two decades ago, it created a sensation and brought him instant fame and fortune. Since then, his creations have been the inspiration for new buildings all over the world.

The Critic Who Couldn't

John Ruskin (1819-1900)
— British writer and art critic —

John Ruskin's parents just didn't know when to let go. His mother taught him at home until he was ready for college, and then she stayed in a hotel off campus to keep an eye on him. (His father came up every weekend to supervise.) Ruskin went on to become a prolific writer and one of the most influential art critics of the nineteenth century. He helped England accept the idea that classical art was not the *only* form of art. But his smothered childhood had left its mark. His wife divorced him after six years of a marriage that was still unconsummated. She happily married one of his artist protégés, but Ruskin lapsed into madness.

When Ugliness is Beauty

John French Sloan (1871-1951)
— *American painter, illustrator, engraver* —

After decades of trying, **John Sloan** finally sold his first painting when he was forty-two years old. Not until he was in his seventies could he finally make a living painting full time. Why? Because his paintings were judged to be too "ugly." His brand of realism irked the critics' sensibilities. In time, though, they came to appreciate the artistic message in Sloan's works. Then ironically, "ugly" was in, and some critics began to complain that Sloan's paintings weren't ugly enough.

CHAPTER 5

JOHN IN THE BUSINESS WORLD

John Akers

Look to the Leader

John Fellows Akers (1934-)
— Chairman & CEO of IBM —

    IBM has always been one of the leaders in the business world. In today's information age, IBM has a key position in the center of the innovations and technological advances making news and reaching into our lives, as everyone tries to keep up with the leader. Talented **John Akers** worked his way up in twenty-five years from sales trainee to chief executive officer of the corporate giant. Akers has been instrumental in guiding his company's growth, and in keeping IBM a few steps ahead of the competition.

New York's Landlord

John Jacob Astor (1763-1848)
— German-American financier —

At one time the Astor family owned more of New York City than anyone else. The family fortune was started by **John Jacob Astor**, a German immigrant who built his fur empire into the nation's first monopoly. He used his money to invest in farmland. That farmland was soon to become the heart of one of the world's most active cities, New York City's Manhattan. When Astor died, he was the richest man in the nation.

Liberal Economist

John Kenneth Galbraith (1908-)
— American economist, diplomat —

President John F. Kennedy was having breakfast one day with his economic adviser, **John Galbraith**. *The New York Times* had done a profile on Galbraith, and Kennedy asked his friend what he thought of it. The economist conceded it was OK, but why did they have to call him arrogant? "I don't see why not," Kennedy answered, "everybody else does." Galbraith, though born in Canada, has had a great influence on economic theory and thought in the United States, especially from the forties through the seventies. His liberal views have often clashed with those of conservative economists, but, as he observes, "they have always endured in the end."

The Oil King

J(ean) Paul Getty (1892-1976)
— *American oil billionaire* —

"Some people find oil. Others don't". That was what **J. Paul Getty** said was the secret to his success. Of course it doesn't hurt if your parents have a lot of money to help you get started, too. Like many other wealthy people, Getty was a little eccentric. Although he was worth *billions*, he had a pay phone installed in his home for guests to use. Today, the numerous Getty oil stations across the world are a constant reminder of the man whose name was synonymous with wealth.

Economic Activist

John Maynard Keynes (1883-1946)
— *British economist* —

With but a single graduate course in economics in his background, **John Maynard Keynes** was asked to teach a basic economics course at Cambridge University. That was how highly they regarded Keynes' ability. He went on to become a dominant figure in economics with the publication of his magnum opus, *General Theory of Employment, Interest, and Money*, in 1936. His recommendation of government intervention to keep the economy on an even keel has been utilized by nations all around the world.

The Million-Dollar Scowl

John L(lewellyn) Lewis (1880-1969)
— *American labor leader* —

At the beginning of the century, the mines were a terrible place to work: dark and dirty and dangerous. It seemed like the owners were only interested in profits. But miner **John L. Lewis** changed all that. Armed with a thundering voice, a bushy-eye-browed scowl, and bulldog determination, this union leader stood up to the mine owners and won concessions that helped not only miners but workers in all the other major industries. Ultimately a wealthy man in his own right, he always kept the common touch and enjoyed his bogeyman image.

36

J.P. Morgan

Financial Giant

J(ohn) P(ierpont) Morgan (1837-1913)
— American financier —

    J. P. Morgan created one of the biggest financial empires ever. As a young man in his early twenties, Morgan, with the help of his parents' money, was well on his way to establishing himself in the business world. But love captured his heart, and he put everything aside to devote himself to his bride, Mimi. She was

37

dying of tuberculosis, and neither Morgan's wealth nor a honey-moon in the sunny Mediterranean could save her. Mimi died in his arms, and Morgan was devastated. In time he recovered and went on to show the world his financial genius as he consolidated smaller competing companies, creating corporate giants like AT&T, General Electric, and U.S. Steel. Those who knew him as the classic plutocrat would never have dreamed he had once been ready to give it all up for love.

The First Billionaire

John Davison Rockefeller (1839-1937)
— *American industrialist, philanthropist* —

At sixteen **John D. Rockefeller** worked in a produce store; by thirty-one he was president of the Standard Oil Company of Ohio and well on his way to becoming the world's first billion-aire. Rockefeller gave new meaning to the words "antitrust" and "monopoly". He eliminated nearly all the opposition in the oil-refining industry, in ways that today would be quite illegal. When Rockefeller retired, he worked as hard at being a philanthropist as he had at being an industrialist. In his last twenty-five years he gave away more than $500 million. When he died at the age of ninety-seven, his estate included only a single share of Standard Oil stock, worth $43.94!

The Customer Is Always Right

John Wanamaker (1838-1922)
— *American merchant, philanthropist, U.S. Cabinet member* —

John Wanamaker was a pioneer. Instead of exploring new territories, he blazed new trails in merchandising. To list his firsts would fill up a book. The store that he founded in Philadel-phia in 1869 was the forerunner of the modern department store, with built-in restaurant, home furnishings, ladies' and other departments, and even the first widespread use of incandescent lighting, just developed by Thomas Edison. John Wanamaker &

Co. brought customers in with clever ads and promotions and kept them with honest value. Wanamaker became a rich and successful businessman and philanthropist.

Out with the Lo Tech in with the Hi Tech

John Francis Welch, Jr. (1935-)
— *CEO of GE* —

"We want to be a company that is constantly renewing itself, shedding the past, adapting to change." These words by General Electric's chairman, **John Welch**, sum up the path GE has taken in the eighties under his direction. Indeed, GE has become a force to be reckoned with. In every major area in which the company is actively involved, it ranks either first or second in sales. Its divisions have become innovative, and the quality of its products has improved dramatically. The development of competent managers by the GE system has become so effective that other companies regularly raid its staff to fill top managerial posts. With this success behind him, Jack Welch is not satisfied — not until GE becomes number one in the nation.

CHAPTER 6

JOHN IN ENTERTAINMENT

A Blues Brother

John Belushi *(1949-1982)*
— American comedian and actor —

In high school **John Belushi** was the true blue All American kid — captain of the football team, homecoming king, and member of the choir, drama team, and debating club. After high school everything seemed to be going right for this "soul man." His zany, off-beat humor tickled America's funnybone on *Saturday Night Live*, and in the movie *The Blues Brothers*. "But noooooooo." John was always known for his fun-loving, frenzied lifestyle. After a few movie "flops," he began to lose control and found himself immersed in a world of drugs. An overdose of cocaine and heroin one evening ended the life of this talented young comedian.

The Penny-Pinching Philanthropist

Jack Benny (Benjamin Kubelsky) *(1894-1974)*
— American comedian —

No history of American comedy would be complete without **Jack Benny**. His start in vaudeville led to his famous radio show that tickled the nation for decades. When he switched to TV in the fifties, he brought with him a large, dedicated audience. His penny-

Jack Benny

pinching stage personality was nothing like the real Jack Benny. He was warm, giving, and always helpful to people in need. Benny's classic comedy lives on in recordings and reruns of his radio and TV shows.

Bard of the Boulevard

John Carradine (Richmond Reed Carradine) (1902-1988)
— American actor —

    John Carradine was one of Hollywood's most colorful character actors, with, as he claimed, nearly 500 movie appearances. These movies ranged from horror films to classics like *The*

Grapes of Wrath and *Captains Courageous,* to the children's classic *The Secret of NIMH.* His powerful voice was perfect for Shakespearean drama, and between films he often performed on stage. Carradine also had a flair for melodrama in his personal life — he earned the sobriquet of the "Bard of the Boulevard" for his habit of strolling the streets of Hollywood dressed in a satin cape, while reciting Shakespeare. Though he advised his sons to avoid the acting profession, David, Keith, and Robert are carrying on this distinguished Carradine tradition.

"Heeeere's .... Johnny"

Johnny Carson (John William Carson) (1925-)
— American talk show host and comedian —
"Heeeere's .... Johnny": one of the most popular television personalities of all time. Since 1962, when **Johnny Carson** first hosted *The Tonight Show,* he and his sidekick Ed McMahon have been known and loved by people across the country. With a viewing audience of over fifteen million, Carson continues to be the King of talk-show hosts. Commenting on *The Tonight Show's* firm standing in late night television, Johnny once said, "We're more effective than birth control."

Dynasty's Patriarch

John Forsythe (John Lincoln Freund) (1918-)
— American actor —
In the role of Blake Carrington, powerful patriarch of the long-running TV series *Dynasty,* **John Forsythe** has achieved fame and fortune — quite an accomplishment for someone who didn't start out as an actor. He dreamed of playing major league baseball and then announced games for the Brooklyn Dodgers before he decided to try acting — only to be told he had no talent! An offer of free acting lessons gave him the chance to gain acting skills, and then there was a long, slow climb up the acting ladder. There were parts on radio soap operas, in movies, Broadway theatre, and finally — *Dynasty*! John Forsythe's life has never been the same since.

42

The Gamblings Ramble On

The Gamblings: John B. (1897-1974), John A. (1930-), & John R. (1950-)
— *American radio announcers* —

The 21st century will be quite different from our world of today — that is, except for the *Rambling with Gambling Show.* Since 1925, three generations of Gamblings have been entertaining radio listeners over two-thirds of the United States on the powerful beam of New York's station WOR. **John B. Gambling** began it all, filling in for the absent announcer of a wake-up show. He and his offspring (**John A.** and his son **John R.**) have been a morning tradition ever since. The Gambling mix of general information, humor, and commentary, interspersed with news and commercials, seems to be just what people need to start the day. It's a good bet that our grandchildren will be waking up to the voice of one of John R.'s three sons after the turn of the century.

The Great One

Jackie Gleason (Herbert John Gleason) (1916-1987)
— *American comedian and actor* —

Jackie Gleason's career went up and down like the size of his clothes. He was a big guy, and a big star. *The Honeymooners,* his claim to fame, ran for only one season and was not successful at the time. Thirty years later, however, it continues to be one of the most popular reruns in the history of television. The Great One, as he was called, immortalized the lines, "How sweet it is," "Baby, you're the greatest," "Pow! Right in the kisser," and "Away we go!" In addition to *The Honeymooners,* Gleason will always be remembered for his dramatic performance in *The Hustler* and *Nothing in Common.*

Hollywood Heavyweight

John Goodman (1952-)
— *American actor* —

Ralph Kramden was **John Goodman**'s favorite TV char-

43

acter, and this 250+ pound actor may someday be as famous as his idol. After playing parts in several 1987 and 1988 movies including *Everybody's All American* and *Punchline*, Goodman became known all across America with the 1988 TV season hit *Roseanne*. He has become so popular that USA Today called this size 54-long, "the New Improved Sexiest Man Alive," and *Playgirl* magazine editor-in-chief Nancie Martin said she wouldn't be surprised to see Goodman in the 1989 "10 sexiest men in America" list.

John Houseman

Professor Kingsfield

John Houseman (Jacques Haussmann) (1902-1988)
— American actor, producer, director, writer —

Although **John Houseman** had a very diverse and remarkably productive life, he will always be remembered as the imperturbable Harvard Law Professor Kingsfield in the 1974 smash hit, *Paper Chase*. Houseman came to America in 1925 and at once displayed his creative talents as a writer and translator of plays from German and French to English, and as producer and director for the stage, the movies, and TV. But his performance in *Paper Chase* changed the direction of his career and immortalized his name as an actor.

A Full Life

John Huston (1906-1987)
— *American movie director, actor, screen writer, soldier, boxer, playwright, reporter, editor, etc.* —

Walter Mitty never lived as many lives vicariously as **John Huston** lived in the real world. Trying dozens of jobs and professions, Huston finally hit upon the one that was to make him world famous: movie directing. As a director he won two Oscars and thirteen Oscar nominations. Enough for any man — except Huston. Had he not died at eighty-one he probably would have worked past 100. Doubtless the two most satisfying movies for him were *The Treasure of the Sierra Madre*, in which both he and his father won Oscars, and *Prizzi's Honor*, for which his daughter, Anjelica, won an Oscar.

Versatile Comedian

Jack Lemmon (John Uhler Lemmon III) (1925-)
— *American actor* —

Jack Lemmon is one of America's great comedic geniuses. He won an Oscar for his performance in *Mister Roberts* and captured everyone's attention in *The Odd Couple*. But he's equally at home with dramas, as well. He won another Oscar for his riveting performance in *Save the Tiger* and kept filmgoers at the edge of their seats in *The China Syndrome* and *Missing*. In recognition of his outstanding abilities, Jack Lemmon became the sixteenth recipient of the American Film Institute's annual and prestigious Life Achievement Award in 1988.

One of A Kind

Jack Nicholson (John Joseph Nicholson (1937-)
— American actor —

Jack Nicholson started his Hollywood career in low-budget thrillers. But after his Oscar-nominated performances in *Easy Rider* and *Five Easy Pieces*, he was well on his way to making a name for himself. Then came his part as a sane man trying to survive in an insane asylum, in *One Flew Over the Cuckoo's Nest*. Nicholson was perfect for the part. He won an Oscar for the role and was catapulted to the top. With his Oscar-winning performance in *Terms of Endearment* and other recent successes in *Prizzi's Honor* and *Batman,* Jack Nicholson continues to captivate his audiences with his unique style.

Rising Star

Sean Penn (1960-)
— American actor —

Sean Penn first attracted attention as an actor to be watched with his 1981 performances in *Taps* and *Fast Times at Ridgemont High*. Since then he has established himself as one of America's most outstanding actors. *Racing With the Moon, The Falcon and the Snowman, At Close Range, Colors and Casualties —* all brought critical acclaim. Newer roles in *We're No Angels* and *State of Grace* should further add to the reputation of this talented actor. Sean Penn's future plans will place him on the other side of the camera, as a film director.

Staying Alive

John Travolta (1954-)
— American actor, dancer, singer —

John Travolta started out his career touring with the road company of the Broadway musical *Grease* in a minor role. Six years later he was a star playing the lead in the smash-hit movie version. Travolta first gained recognition in the TV show *Welcome Back, Kotter*. By the time he became a superstar with his Academy Award nominated performance in *Saturday Night Fever* he had

46

already made a name for himself singing on records. In later movies, including some serious dramatic roles and the 1989 surprise hit, *Look Who's Talking,* John Travolta has continued to display fine acting abilities along with his good looks.

Midnight Cowboy

Jon Voight (1938-)
— American actor —

Most men, if given the chance, would love to act in the movies in the role of a handsome, ne'er-do-wrong hero. **Jon Voight**, after his smash hit, *Midnight Cowboy*, has constantly sought out roles that portray a "hero" with a serious fault — roles that would challenge the talents of even the best actors. Jon certainly has succeeded. His Oscar for his sensitive portrayal of a paraplegic Vietnam veteran in *Coming Home* will undoubtedly be the first of several.

John Wayne

47

Star of the Wild West

John Wayne (Marion Michael Morrison) (1907-1979)
— *American actor* —

Some people claim that **John Wayne**, the all-time greatest Western star, was very limited in his acting roles. "I play John Wayne in every part regardless of the character, and I've been doing okay, haven't I?" He did more than okay. For over twenty-five years, John Wayne was one of Hollywood's top money-making attractions. He made more than 250 films over a span of forty years in the movie industry. John Wayne created an image of the true American — strong, silent, courageous. His own life reflected this image. For over fifteen years he quietly battled cancer; when he died, a Congressional Medal was struck in his honor.

The Father of Improvisation

Jonathan (Harshman) Winters (1925-)
— *American comedian, actor, disc jockey, painter, writer* —

Jonathan Winters is quite a comedian with a loyal following. He is a genius at portraying comedic characters with odd personalities and getting laughs where others would get blank stares. He gained worldwide recognition in *It's A Mad, Mad, Mad, Mad World,* and has delighted his fans with thousands of guest appearances on TV shows, including frequent visits to *The Tonight Show.* He was also the star of three of his own shows in the fifties, sixties, and seventies, played Mork and Mindy's hatched son, and made a dozen movies. Jonathan Winters' inventive style of humor won him a reputation as "The Father of Improvisation" in the 1960s. This comedian is also an accomplished painter and had a surprise best-selling book, the *1988 Winters' Tales.* Ironically Random House agreed to publish the book mainly because they wanted the autobiography he was working on, *I Couldn't Wait For Success — I Went On Ahead Without It.*

48

CHAPTER 7

JOHN IN HISTORY

Johnny Appleseed

Jonathan Chapman (1774-1845)
— American missionary nurseryman —

There really was a man who traveled across America planting apple trees wherever he went. From coast to coast, **Jonathan Chapman** roamed barefoot with a tin pot on his head, bringing news, stories, and medical help to many a weary and lonely frontiersman. He left behind a lot more than just the apple tree orchards he planted. Legends grew and flourished, and soon no one knew for sure which tales were true and which were embellished. Still, one thing is certain — the all-American fruit, the apple, owes a good deal of its popularity to that great American folk hero, Johnny Appleseed.

Rabble-Rouser or Hero?

John Brown (1800-1859)
— American abolitionist —

There are people who feel it is improper to kill for any cause. There are others who regard rebels as heroes, idolizing those who have gladly given their lives or killed for a cause they believed in. **John Brown** was a rebel. A white man who

John Brown

believed in the brotherhood of men of all colors, he killed for his cause: the liberation of the enslaved Negroes in the South. In his last historic raid, he and twenty-one other men captured the U.S. arsenal at Harper's Ferry. He paid with his life, but his story inspired the Union soldiers in the song, "John Brown's Body." Ironically, the capturing officer who led a troop of U.S. Marines against him was Robert E. Lee.

After Columbus

John Cabot (Giovanni Caboto) (1450-c1498)
— Italian-English explorer —
Christopher Columbus discovered America in 1492, but

how did America become a British colony? While Columbus was thinking of reaching the Orient by traveling West, another Italian explorer, Giovanni Caboto, came up with similar ideas. He moved his family to England in 1484, changed his name to **John Cabot**, and set about seeking support for a transatlantic journey. In 1494 he set out; he landed in New Foundland, and, like Columbus, thought he had reached the Orient. The ships he took out on a second voyage never returned, but Cabot's explorations paved the way for English colonization of the New World.

An American in Orbit

John Herschell Glenn (1921-)
— American astronaut, U.S. Senator —

Not everyone has what it takes to be an astronaut. They're a special breed, willing to venture out into the unknown voids of space, far from every form of life as we know it. **John Glenn** has all the right stuff. In 1962 he became the first American to orbit our planet. His safe return to Earth, after a technical malfunction, was a dramatic episode that had the nation holding its breath. John Glenn became a national hero, and twenty-two years later he made a serious bid for the Presidency of the United States. Although unsuccessful in that campaign, he has continued to serve his country as the conscientious and capable Senator from Ohio since 1974.

The Printed Word

Johann Gutenberg (Johann Gensfleisch zur Laden zum Gutenberg) (c1394-1468)
— German goldsmith, inventor —

We live in a technological society, where information is king. Until the recent invention of electronic media, knowledge was recorded and transferred by way of the printed word. **Johann Gutenberg** was the one who made it all possible. Best remembered for the first printed work, the *Gutenberg Bible*, he modified a winepress to create the first printing press with movable type.

51

Johann Gutenberg

Gutenberg got little from his invention other than personal satisfaction. Borrowing for the venture, he went in over his head and eventually lost everything to his backer, Johann Fust.

Mr. FBI

J(ohn) Edgar Hoover (1895-1972)
— American Director of the FBI —

For almost fifty years **J. Edgar Hoover** *was* the FBI. Before he became its director in 1924, the FBI was a small and inefficient Federal agency. Hoover built it into one of the world's most prestigious and efficient ones. He was so powerful, Presidents tolerated his arrogance, not daring to attempt his ouster. Hoover practically hand-picked the country's best law enforcement agents and instilled in them total loyalty to the "chief." Under Hoover's direction an FBI academy and a state-of-the-art crime lab were set up, and the world's largest fingerprint file was established.

A Future President?

Jack French Kemp (1935-)
— U.S. Congressman, professional football player —
Some people think **Jack Kemp** will be President of the United States one day. Intelligent, charismatic, and determined, he is a former star quarterback who set passing and completion records in the American Football League. His number "15" was retired by the Buffalo Bills in commemoration of his outstanding achievements. Kemp found life after football in Congress. His supply-side economics, instituted during the Reagan Administration, is still influencing our economy today. Now, at the helm of the Department of Housing and Urban Development, Kemp is facing the challenge of finding ways to house the homeless and revive the American dream of affordable housing.

Pirate or National Hero?

Jean Lafitte (1780-1825?)
— French pirate —
If Americans can glorify gunmen and gangsters, then why not a pirate? **Jean Lafitte** became a national hero after he and his men fought heroically against the British outside New Orleans during the War of 1812. For this the former pirates received full pardons. But the life of an honest man didn't agree with Lafitte, so he returned to his pirate ways. His men disobeyed his orders never to attack American ships, and the U.S. lost patience with him. He was forced to flee to the Spanish Main — and was never heard from again.

53

Death at the Fountain of Youth

Juan Ponce de Leon (1460-1521)
— Spanish explorer —

Few explorers have captured the imagination of the public as has **Juan Ponce de Leon**. Mention his name, and "Fountain of Youth" springs to mind. Yet he never found the mythical fountain, although he discovered a beautiful "island" that he named "Florida." It was there that he received his death blow. On his return to the coast of Florida, eight years after his historic discovery of this peninsula, Ponce de Leon was ambushed by unfriendly Indians and fatally wounded. He died in Cuba shortly afterward, but his memory lives on in Puerto Rico's third largest city: Ponce.

John Smith

Colonial Adventurer

John Smith *(1580-1631)*
— *English explorer* —

If even a quarter of the tales told by explorer **John Smith** were true, he led a fantastic life. An apprentice merchant, mercenary soldier, Turkish slave, and mutineer: that was his background when he was chosen to organize the first permanent English settlement at Jamestown, Virginia. He put the new village on its feet, but while exploring the wilderness, he was nearly killed by unfriendly Indians. No sooner did he escape, with the aid of an Indian princess, than he was arrested by the colonists and sentenced to death for losing the men on his expedition. He got out of that predicament, too, and survived to reminisce and write about his New World adventures.

The Truth Is Eternal

John Peter Zenger *(1697-1746)*
— *Colonial American printer* —

In colonial times newspapers had to be careful whom they attacked. If the injured party was powerful enough, the writer would be found guilty of libel — irrespective of the truth of the printed material. The trial of **John Zenger** changed all that. He was imprisoned for printing statements against Governor Cosby, the colonial governor of New York. He spent ten months in jail, while his wife bravely carried on the publication of his weekly newspaper. Although the judge was prejudiced against him, Zenger won his case with the aid of a brilliant Philadelphia lawyer, Andrew Hamilton. Zenger's courageous crusade secured the freedom of the press for future generations.

55

CHAPTER 8

JOHN IN LITERATURE

Tales That Live

Hans Christian Andersen (1805-1875)
— *Danish writer* —

Some of the most beautiful tales in print were written by a real-life ugly duckling. People laughed at him, saying he looked more like a stork than a man, with his long nose and thin, gangling body. But **Hans Christian Andersen** has enthralled generations of children and adults. From *The Ugly Duckling* to *The Red Shoes,* his stories have been translated into over a hundred languages and have become part of our Western culture. Andersen spent much of his life visiting famous friends like novelist Charles Dickens. He never married, but carried a letter from his first love in a small leather bag suspended around his neck. When he died, in compliance with his will, it was destroyed — unread.

The Father of Italian Prose

Giovanni Boccaccio (1313-1375)
— *Italian writer* —

Before **Boccaccio,** serious literature was written mostly in Latin poetic verses. Through his influence, writing in common, ordinary language became an accepted medium for literary masterpieces. His poems, short stories, and novels were so innovative that they influenced many later literary giants. Shakespeare's *Romeo and Juliet,* for example, is based on a Boccaccio short story. Boccaccio's greatest achievement was *Decameron,* a collection of 100 interwoven short stories. In the book seven young women and three young men have taken refuge from the Plague in a deserted villa. Each day one is chosen as the King or Queen for the day. For ten days each of the refugees tells a story based on a subject chosen by that day's leader.

He Gave Them Their Start

John W(ood) Campbell *(1910-1971)*
— American science fiction writer, editor —

Isaac Asimov, Robert Heinlein, Theodore Sturgeon — the list reads like a who's who of science fiction. John Campbell discovered them all, and many more. As editor of *Astounding* (later, *Analog*) magazine, he played a key role in the development of many of today's science fiction stars and helped to shape the genre for a generation. He was opinionated, and his ideas were often off beat, but they were always worth listening to. A talented writer in his own right, Campbell is better remembered as the paragon of a science fiction editor.

No Man Is an Island

John Donne *(1572-1631)*
— English poet, priest —

John Donne was a gifted and creative poet. But a narrow-minded monarch, King James I, forced him to take on a full-time job as an Anglican clergyman. Donne had little choice, for he had married for love, and his wife and dozen children were threatened with starvation. How much beauty the world has lost will never be known, but the price was surely too great to pay. For the next seventeen years — the rest of his life — hardly a line of nonreligious poetry was written by this rare talent.

The Age of Dryden

John Dryden (1631-1700)
— *British poet, playwright* —

John Dryden was the dominant literary figure of his day. And yet, because of politics, he was forced to eke out a living in his prime. In his younger years, Dryden was able to move with the times, though they were constantly changing. He wrote for Oliver Cromwell, but when Charles II was restored to the throne he wrote poems in praise of the King. When a Roman Catholic, James II, gained the throne, Dryden converted to Catholicism to remain in favor. But in 1688, when the Protestants William and Mary came into power, Dryden held firm to his Catholic beliefs and lost his positions as poet laureate and royal historiographer, as well as his pension.

Dull Bond?

Ian Lancaster Fleming (1908-1964)
— *British writer, journalist* —

James Bond, dull? To any 007 fan that would seem impossible. Yet **Ian Fleming** originally planned Bond as a dull person to whom unusual things happened. Few heroes in literature are as dynamic, resourceful, and charismatic as 007, whose creator drew on his own experiences as a real-life intelligence agent. Bond leaped to stardom in 1961, shortly after the release of the first 007 movie, when President Kennedy said he was an avid James Bond fan. It is a pity that Ian Fleming did not live much beyond this date, to see his creation take the world by storm. Every one of the original Bond books has been translated into a successful movie, and the Bond cult has taken on a life of its own.

Creator of Faust

Johann Wolfgang von Goethe (1749-1832)
— *German poet, playwright, and novelist* —

Johann Goethe was the German version of Leonardo da

Johann Wolfgang von Goethe

Vinci — a Renaissance man with wide-ranging interests and over-flowing brilliance. He is remembered as a literary genius, ranked by some on a par with Shakespeare and Homer. From his youthful romantic novel, *The Sorrows of Young Werther,* which was the rage of Europe, to his mature masterpiece, *Faust,* an enduring classic, Goethe was productive for most of his eighty-two years. Not only writer, though, he was also a songwriter, amateur painter, a scholar and critic of art history, philosopher, scientist, and statesman.

The Old Wild West Lives

Zane Grey (1872-1939)
— American writer —

    For decades Westerns filled the screens of movie houses throughout the nation, as millions of "hooked" fans lived briefly in fantasy worlds of frontier times. **Zane Grey** had a great deal to do with that phase of American tastes and fantasies. His Westerns, written in the early part of this century, are classics and set the tone for a whole genre of literature.

Prolific American Writer

Evan Hunter (1926-)
— American writer —

    The 1955 movie *Blackboard Jungle* was a milestone in movie history. It was based on the extremely popular first novel by **Evan Hunter,** which made him an "overnight success" — although he had already had a hundred stories published. Since then this prolific writer has gone on to create dozens of successful novels, as well as movie screenplays, like the classic Hitchcock thriller, *The Birds.* But Hunter is also the author behind the 87th Precinct crime series, written under his pseudonym Ed McBain. *Newsweek* called one of these novels, *Ice,* one of the ten best crime novels of the twentieth century.

He Died Too Soon

John Keats (1795-1821)
— British poet —

    The world will never know what beauty was lost because English poet **John Keats** unselfishly cared for his dying brother. His bitter reward was tuberculosis and death at the age of twenty-five. Keats wrote his greatest works while he was dying. Though critics had ridiculed some of his early poems, his last book of poetry was well received when it appeared in 1820. In his brief career Keats created a small but shining legacy, which had a deep impact

John Keats

on the style of generations of poets that followed. It was a splendid denial of the epitaph carved on his tombstone: "Here lies one whose name is writ on water."

Call of the Wild

Jack London (John Griffith Chaney) (1876-1916)
— American writer —

No other dog story ever written has had the impact of **Jack London's** *Call of the Wild.* It has been translated into dozens of languages; millions of children have grown up with it. Jack London led a full but short life. He was arrested for vagrancy, was shot at during the Russo-Japanese War, sailed around the world, and rose from poverty to be the highest paid writer in America, only to lose it all in spendthrift abandon that ended in suicide. This great American's life was as wild and untamed as many of the characters in the fifty books published during his seventeen-year literary career.

Cold, Insensitive, Brilliant, and Insightful

John Milton *(1608-1674)*
— British poet, political writer —

John Milton was a paradox. He could mold verse with a sensitive brilliance that few have ever equaled. But in his relations with his fellow humans — most especially with his own family —he was tactless, stubborn, and callous. *Paradise Lost,* a monumental work that Milton completed while totally blind, stands as one of the most magnificent works of poetry ever penned. This and his other two epic poems, *Paradise Regained* and *Samson Agonistes,* were written at the end of a brilliant literary career that was interspersed with political machinations, unhappy marriages, and a virtual enslavement of his three daughters. A failure as a man, perhaps; but Milton's place among the literary greats is secure.

Greatest French Comedian

Molière (Jean-Baptiste Poquelin) *(1622-1673)*
— French actor, director, stage manager, playwright —

Classic comedian Charlie Chaplin was once called "the best comic since **Molière**." This is quite a tribute to someone who lived three hundred years ago. But Molière's comedic genius went beyond acting. He wrote much of his material, and his writing style and content set standards that have held for centuries. His ability to satirize the frailties of people, especially the VIPs of his time, has been unequaled in French drama — and perhaps that of the world.

Molière (Jean-Baptiste Poquelin)

An Irish Patriot

Sean O'Casey (John Casey) (1880-1964)
— *Irish playwright* —

When humor cannot be treated as humor but becomes the focus of accusations of prejudice, we know the human disease of intolerance has gone too far. Today, ethnic jokes provoke scathing denunciation. In the 1920s, a true Irish patriot, **Sean O'Casey,** was accused of treason because his witty plays appeared to poke fun at some Irish revolutionary heroes. Sean left Ireland in disgust and disillusionment. He went to England, where he continued to write plays and worked hard for world peace.

The Grapes of Wrath

John Steinbeck (1902-1968)
— *American writer* —

   John Steinbeck is one of America's greatest writers. He won a Pulitzer Prize for *The Grapes of Wrath* and a Nobel Prize for *The Winter of Our Discontent.* He was fired from his first real job as a reporter in New York because he insisted on coloring his reporting of the underprivileged with a highly sympathetic slant — a trait that was to persist throughout his literary career. Before his books became popular enough to bring in a decent living, Steinbeck supported himself as a bricklayer, a chemist, and a painter's apprentice. These experiences provided him with authentic backgrounds for the struggling characters that would make him famous.

Gulliver's Satirist

Jonathan Swift (1667-1745)
— *British (Irish) satirist and clergyman* —

   Taken at face value, **Jonathan Swift**'s *A Modest Proposal* was monstrous. His suggestion that poor Irish peasants offer their children as a source of food for the rich who were preying upon them was not, of course, meant to be taken at face value, but as a biting satire. Swift was constantly calling the public's attention to the frailties and injustices of the world of his day. *Gulliver's Travels,* read as a children's story for more than two centuries, is a watered-down version of Swift's most famous multilayered satire of his society.

Living Literary Influence

John Updike (1932-)
— *American writer* —

   One of the most frequent contributors to *The New Yorker* magazine is **John Updike.** He has written many short stories, poems, humorous essays, and book reviews, as well as fourteen novels. The culmination of his literary influence was reached in 1982 with the award of the Pulitzer Prize for his novel, *Rabbit Is Rich*. Updike continues to be an active contributor to the literary scene as he explores the life and concerns of, primarily, small-town, middle-class America.

CHAPTER 9

JOHN IN MUSIC

Johann Sebastian Bach

First of the "Three B's"

Johann Sebastian Bach *(1685-1750)*
— *German composer, teacher, conductor* —
    Johann Sebastian Bach was no stranger to frustration.

He produced eight hundred musical creations, but they were virtually unappreciated during his lifetime. Meanwhile the works of others — including two of Bach's own sons — were lauded by the critics of his day. It was only after his death — indeed, more than fifty years later — that the true genius of Bach began to be understood. This appreciation has continued to grow with the passage of time until today he is ranked among the all-time greats of classical music. Indeed, he is the first of the famous "three B's": Bach, Beethoven, and Brahms.

Dollar Bills in Heavy Metal

Jon Bon Jovi (John Bongiovi) (1962-)
— American singer, musician, composer —

Hard rock turns some people off, but it turns quite a few people on. Among the leaders of the heavy metal music scene is **Jon Bon Jovi.** His stream of hit songs has rocketed him to the top of the charts again and again. *Slippery When Wet* (1986) sold an impressive thirteen million copies in a single year. Not bad for a young man who got his start sweeping floors in a cousin's recording studio! His fans may seem to lose their control at times, as his group puts on their shows, but Bon Jovi has excellent control over an obviously exciting future.

Star-Crossed Romantic

Johannes Brahms *(1833-1897)*
— German composer and pianist —

Meeting the right people can have a big effect on a career. **Johannes Brahms** was lucky in his friends: violinist Joseph Joachim introduced him to the superstars of the day, and influential composer Robert Schumann took the young Brahms under his wing. Schumann's sponsorship brought his protege early fame, and Schumann's wife Clara became the unrequited love of Brahms' life. His thwarted passions found expression in music as he became a leader of the nineteenth century German romantic movement.

67

Brahm's four symphonies, piano and violin concertos, and his choral work, *A German Requiem,* earned him a place among classical music's great "three B's."

World In Motion

Jackson Browne (1950-)
— *American singer, songwriter, musician* —

Jackson Browne is considered by many as the greatest male "song poet" of the seventies. While still in high school he was offered a record contract to write songs. He left his home in LA and headed for New York, where he sang at folk festivals. It wasn't long before other artists, like Linda Ronstadt, Tom Rush, and the Byrds, were singing Jackson Browne songs. Finally Browne broke through as a performer with a single from his first album, *Doctor My Eyes,* released in 1971. The next year a song he wrote with Glen Frey, *Take It Easy,* launched a new group called the Eagles to stardom. Browne's blend of folk, country and rock and his leading role in the No-Nukes movement in the seventies helped create a large and loyal following. His continuing social concern is reflected in his provocative 1989 album, *World In Motion.*

Natural Music

John Cage (1912-)
— *American composer* —

John Cage's creative and radical musical ideas have had an enormous impact on contemporary music, art, dance and theater. For over fifty years Cage has experimented in musical ventures that have built on his philosophy that music is everywhere all around us — but only if the listener is in tune to it. An audience should not listen only for the particular notes a composer has selected, but should experience all of the sounds that take place during each unique performance. His most familiar compositions, *4'33",* in which a pianist sits for four minutes and thirty-three seconds not playing, and *Imaginary Landscapes No. 4,* for a conductor, twenty-four players and twelve randomly tuned radios, are perfect examples of his attempts to capture the music that comes from the randomness of nature.

John Cage

The Man In Black

Johnny Cash (1932-)
— American country singer, actor —

Johnny Cash is one of the most enduring of all present-day entertainment greats. In a career that spans nearly thirty-five years, he has recorded almost 1500 songs on over 470 albums, and sold over fifty million records worldwide. His universal appeal has made him in demand from L.A. to London, from the Boston Pops to the Grand Ole Opry, from Budapest to Paris, from Cuba to Vegas, from *Sesame Street* to Carnegie Hall, from Alaska to Australia, from the White House to Folsom Prison. Johnny Cash's straightforward, grass-roots delivery of song has carved this "Man In Black" an everlasting niche in the history of American music.

John Denver

Rocky Mountain Denver

John Denver (Henry John Deutschendorf, Jr.) (1943-)
— American singer, songwriter, actor, activist —

     Peter, Paul, and Mary first sang *Leaving On A Jet Plane* in 1969 and rode it to the top of the charts. But it was **John Denver**'s song and it helped launch his career. The years that followed brought many smash hits like *Rocky Mountain High* and *Take Me Home, Country Roads*. Denver also tried his hand at acting, starring with George Burns in the popular movie, *Oh God*. With all his success, John Denver found time to be active in causes such as the antiwar and antihunger movements. In the eighties, he dispensed with his gold-rimmed "granny glasses" and cut his long hair for a new, sexier image. Once called the "Sunshine Boy" and

70

"Tom Sawyer of Rock" because of his wholesome image, John Denver has treated his fans of the eighties to a matured artist, and his music continues to receive praises for its passion and expressiveness.

The First Beatle

John Lennon (1940-1980)
— *British songwriter, musician* —

Assassinations happen to VIPs; for ordinary people it's called murder. **John Lennon** was assassinated on December 8, 1980. One hundred thousand grieving people gathered in New York City's Central Park, and many thousands more came together in cities throughout the world to mourn him. John Lennon was the founder of the group that was to become the Beatles, the trailblazer in rock-n-roll music of the sixties and seventies. The Lennon-McCartney team composed hit after hit that set the course of music for two decades and probably will influence music for generations to come. After the split-up of the Beatles and some years of regrouping, John and his wife, Yoko Ono, were just beginning a new phase of musical innovation when fate struck in the form of an assassin's bullet.

"Wonderful, Wonderful"

Johnny Mathis (John Royce Mathis) (1935-)
— *American singer* —

When **Johnny Mathis** was attending San Francisco State University, the well-known track star had visions of becoming a physical education teacher. But in 1956 he received two invitations, one of which was to change his life. He was invited to participate in the Olympic trials, and Columbia Records offered him a record contract the same week. He chose a musical career, and the world is richer for it. His early fifties and sixties Top Ten chart hits, such as *Chances Are, Wonderful, Wonderful,* and *12th of Never,* are still classics today. This unique and unforgettable singer is a contemporary concert favorite who continues to record several albums a year for Columbia.

71

Genius of American Opera

Gian-Carlo Menotti *(1911-)*
— Italian American operatic composer —

For years American opera was never as popular as operas by European composers. **Gian-Carlo Menotti** helped bridge the gap. Although Italian-born, he lives in the United States and is considered an American composer. Menotti has become the most famous operatic composer of his time. He began composing music at the age of six, and by eleven he had written his first opera. His family brought him to America to study music as a teenager. In his prolific career Menotti composed several popular works and earned two Pulitzer Prizes. One of his most popular pieces was the first opera composed for television, *Amahl and the Night Visitors,* which was first televised on Christmas Eve in 1951 and has been broadcast every year since then.

Johann Wolfgang Amadeus Mozart

Child Prodigy

(Johann Chrysostom) Wolfgang Amadeus Mozart (1756-1791)
— Austrian composer —

Johann Wolfgang Amadeus Mozart was a classic example of a child prodigy. At the age of three he was already demonstrating signs of remarkable musical talent. He was composing music at five, and at six he made his musical debut. As a child he performed before the Kings and Queens of Europe, receiving praise wherever he went. Perhaps it was all this early excitement and attention that led to many ʋf Mozart's problems as an adult. He spent far more than he ever made. His debts mounted daily, and at his death at thirty-five they were monumental. This is all the more surprising, since in his short life Mozart produced more than 600 musical gems that have made him one of the all-time greats of classical music.

Rock 'N Soul Star

John Oates (1948-)
— American singer, songwriter —

Hall and Oates' unique blend of rock and soul music has helped make them the all-time best-selling music duo ever, with sales of over forty million records. They led the music industry in the 1980s with twenty-two Top 40 hits. Songs like *Private Eyes, Kiss On My List, Sara Smile,* and *You've Lost That Lovin' Feeling* have brought Daryl Hall and **John Oates** six platinum albums and eight number one songs. A lot of work goes into making a hit song. In addition to the actual singing, John Oates is an integral part behind the scenes as cowriter and producer of Hall and Oates hits. Offstage, John Oates and his wife, actress Nancy Hunter, enjoy their privacy. And music isn't his only interest. This multidimensional star is an avid tennis player and skier, and an instrument-rated pilot.

Music to March By

John Philip Sousa (1854-1932)
— American composer, bandmaster —

The Stars and Stripes Forever is as much Americana as apple

73

pie and hot dogs. **John Philip Sousa** has broadened a whole dimension of music in our national repertoire: march music. He is unmatched in his contributions in this area. As the head of the U.S. Marine band for twelve years (1880-1892), he was able to "field test" many of his marches. During that span of time he also transformed the band into a world-renowned instrumental group. All together, he composed 140 military marches and deserves the name of "March King."

The Blue Danube

Johann Strauss (1825-1899)
— Austrian composer, conductor —

Mention waltz, and **Johann Strauss** comes to mind. It is not surprising that he is known as the "Waltz King" when you realize that he has composed over 150 waltzes, including his most famous *Blue Danube*. This melodious waltz is probably one of the most widely played musical pieces in history. It is ironic, and sad, that we owe our treasured store of beautiful Strauss waltzes to the early and sudden death of Johann Strauss's father. The elder Johann Strauss, who was a renowned composer of waltzes and an internationally acclaimed conductor, specifically forbade his son to follow in his footsteps. It was only after his death that the younger Strauss, who had taken music lessons secretly, was able to demonstrate to the world his special and brilliant talents.

Close Encounters of the Musical Kind

John T. Williams (1932-)
— U.S. composer, conductor —

The right background music can turn a good movie into a great one. No one knows this, or does it, better than **John Williams.** He has created the film scores for more than sixty-five movies, and he has won four Academy Awards (with twenty-four Oscar nominations) and fifteen Grammy Awards. His hit scores have included the sound tracks for *Jaws, Close Encounters of the*

Third Kind, Superman, Raiders of the Lost Ark, Star Wars, and *ET.* The versatile composer has also written several concert symphonies and concertos. In 1980 Williams was chosen as conductor of the Boston Pops Orchestra, the replacement for Mr. Pops — Arthur Fiedler.

———

CHAPTER 10

JOHN IN RELIGION AND PHILOSOPHY

John Calvin

The Calvin of Calvinism

John Calvin (Jean Cauvin) *(1509-1564)*
— French/Swiss theologian, ecclesiastical statesman —
   It takes a strong faith to be a good Calvinist. Knowing that

no amount of good works will get you into Heaven, you are expected, nonetheless, to perform these good works throughout your life. According to Calvinism, a person's destiny is predetermined at birth, and no one and nothing can undo it. **John Calvin** was only twenty-seven when he wrote his magnum opus, *Institutes of the Christian Religion* (1536), which formed the basis of Calvinism. It set down a new theology that was to sweep throughout Europe, and then much of the world, directly and indirectly affecting the lives of a large fraction of the earth's population. From his base in Geneva, Calvin nurtured this new movement; when he died, in 1564, the fire ignited by his ideas had already spread too far ever to be contained.

St. John the Divine

Saint John the Apostle (first century A.D.)
— *Apostle* —

St. **John the Apostle** was one of the most trusted of the twelve apostles. It was he who was entrusted with the safekeeping of Mary, mother of Jesus. He was with Jesus during the infamous trial, and during the crucifixion. After the death of Jesus, he carried the faith far and wide, for he was "the one whom Jesus loved."

Prepare Ye the Way . . .

John The Baptist (about 7 B.C.)
— *Jewish prophet* —

Jesus was but a young man when he heard that his cousin, **John the Baptist,** was baptizing those who wished to demonstrate their submission to God. So Jesus went, and was baptized in the waters of the Jordan River. Later, after John spoke out against the marriage of the Jewish ruler, King Herod, to Herodias, as a sin against the Jewish law, he was cruelly punished. He was beheaded and his head delivered to the daughter of the new Queen. John the Baptist is remembered and revered by Christians as the prophet who announced the coming of Jesus Christ, the long-awaited messiah.

Pope John Paul II

Catholic Champion of Freedom and the Family

Pope John Paul II (Karol Jozef Wojtyla) (1920-)
— first Polish Pope —

    John Paul II was the first non-Italian pope in 456 years! Polish people all over the world delighted in the fact that he was the first Pole ever to be elected as pope. His brilliant background — he speaks nearly a dozen languages and has two doctorates — and his charismatic presence make him a most impressive senior spokesman for the Catholic faith. But his willingness to press for freedom in totalitarian countries was doubtless responsible for the nearly successful attempt to assassinate him in 1981. The Catholic faith is in the midst of deep controversy, in a world plagued by numerous crises. The strong leadership of Pope John Paul II is fortunate for Catholicism in these trying times.

True Friendship

Jonathan (c1046 B.C.-c1000 B.C.)
— heir to the throne of Israel, son of King Saul —
Jonathan, heir to the throne of Israel, could have been jealous of the young giant-killer, David. Instead, they became close friends, and Jonathan willingly offered his crown to David. Later, he saved David's life by warning him of a plot by his father, King Saul, who was jealous of David's popularity. Only Jonathan's death on the battlefield ended one of history's closest and most memorable friendships.

Life, Liberty, and the Pursuit of Happiness

John Locke (1632-1704)
— English political, educational, and scientific philosopher —
John Locke's ideas have had a profound influence on the world's history. Both the American and French Revolutions were inspired by concepts he had expressed a century earlier. The fundamental rights to "life, liberty, and the pursuit of happiness" were at the basis of Locke's philosophy. His life itself provides another inspiration to those who have reached middle age without yet achieving their goals and dreams. After decades in undistinguished posts as a teacher, physician, and minor bureaucrat, Locke wrote most of his greatest works when he was in his late fifties and sixties.

He Never Was a Boy

John Stuart Mill (1806-1873)
— British philosopher, political economist —
John Stuart Mill said, "I never was a boy." His father, a

brilliant philosopher and director of the East India Company, was his teacher, and a very tough one. Little John began to study Greek, English, and mathematics at three. By seven he was reading Plato in Greek. At seventeen he became a clerk in the East India Company, and he worked hard until he became its director thirty-one years later. Meanwhile, John Stuart Mill pursued an equally successful life of the mind, writing in support of the women's suffrage movement, as well as in the political, scientific, and economic arenas. In his private life, Mill's patience and perseverance eventually brought happiness: After a twenty-one-year platonic relationship with the invalid wife of another man, the two were finally married in 1851 after her husband died.

Social Contract for Revolution

Jean-Jacques Rousseau (1712-1778)
— French philosopher, writer, political theorist —

"Man is born free and everywhere he is in chains." This and other thoughts on freedom as they appeared in **Jean-Jacques Rousseau**'s classic *Social Contract,* provided the rallying focus for the French revolution. His romantic novels influenced literary style for generations. Rousseau's life was a constant battle against guilt, as he blamed himself for the death of his mother, who had died giving birth to him. Perhaps this guilt provided the driving force that led to his outpouring of creative writings and trailblazing philosophy.

In Love for Life

Jean-Paul Sartre (1905-1980)
— French author, philosopher —

It is ironic that **Jean-Paul Sartre,** who originated a philosophy that says life is meaningless, was involved in one of the deepest, most enduring love affairs in history — a fifty-year relationship with noted author Simone de Beauvoir. Sartre was the founder of existentialism, a philosophy whose essence was ex-

pressed in his masterpiece, *Being and Nothingness* (1956). To say
that life is meaningless and then spend your whole life trying to
improve the lot of the downtrodden is another irony that empha-
sizes the complex and brilliant essence of Sartre.

Fate

John Wesley (1703-1791)
— Anglican clergyman, evangelist —

Fate plays strange tricks. As a child, **John Wesley** was
miraculously saved from a fire — an act of God, he felt, that he
must dedicate his life to justifying. Years later, as an Anglican
clergyman visiting America, he fell in love with Sophia Hopkey.
She spurned his love, and complications forced Wesley to flee to
England. If he had won Sophia's love and married her, one of
today's great religions might never have been founded. Instead, in
the more familiar surroundings of his homeland, Wesley organized
the framework of the Methodist faith.

CHAPTER 11

JOHN IN SCIENCE

Breakthrough in Superconductivity

Johannes Georg Bednorz (1950-)
— German scientist —

"Superconductivity" will someday be a term as well known as "computer" is today — it will completely change our society. Superconductivity occurs when a current flows without any loss of power. One of the pioneers in superconductivity is **Johannes Bednorz,** an IBM researcher who ironically won the 1987 Nobel Prize in Physics in his first job after earning his Ph.D. Bednorz and his colleague Karl Muller made a landmark breakthrough in superconductivity that will transform our applications of electricity and technology, with faster computers, trains, cars, planes, and new forms of electronic "magic."

He Filled the World with Atoms

John Dalton (1766-1844)
— English scientist, teacher —

John Dalton's contribution to society is one of the most profound imaginable. This self-taught scientist brought new insight into what the world is made of: the fact that all matter is made up of tiny, indestructible particles called atoms. Dalton did

John Dalton

not coin the word "atom;" that was done two thousand years before by the Greek philosopher, Democritus. But Dalton demonstrated the existence of atoms beyond reasonable doubt and gave rise to a burst of scientific investigation and discovery that continues to this very day and is helping to make the world a better place to live.

The Great Mathematician

(Johann Friedrich) Carl Gauss (1777-1855)
— German mathematician, astronomer —

Gauss was one of the greatest mathematicians of all time, and yet the foundations for most of his mathematical breakthroughs were laid before he was seventeen. At twenty-four he published his theory of numbers, which is considered one of the most brilliant achievements in mathematics. That year he put his mathematical skills to good use. The world's first asteroid, Ceres, had just been discovered, but astronomers were unable to plot its orbit, even after observing it for forty days. After making just three observations, Gauss was able to work out the calculations. When he died a medal was struck in his honor, and a statue of him still stands in the German town of Brunswick, where he was born.

Johannes Kepler

Order in the Heavens

Johannes Kepler (1571-1630)
— *German astronomer* —

Johannes Kepler couldn't have timed his birth better if he had planned it. Just before he was born, Copernicus had shown that the planets revolved around the sun. Tycho Brahe, the great astronomer, had spent his life collecting data about the positions of the stars and planets. When he died, Kepler, who had taken over his position, inherited these precious records. Kepler used them, along with some brilliant insights of his own, to determine the laws of planetary motion — an accomplishment for which he received everlasting fame.

He Discovered How Candy Gives You Energy

Sir Hans Adolph Krebs (1900-1981)
— *German-born British biochemist* —

Few chemical reactions that take place in our bodies are as important as those that produce the energy-rich ATP molecules. If the production of this vital energy source were to stop for just a few minutes, we would die instantly. Medical researcher **Hans Krebs** fled from Nazi Germany to England and began studies that unraveled the energy-producing reactions in the body, now known as the Krebs cycle. In addition to winning the Nobel Prize for this work, Krebs won the prestigious Copley Medal from the Royal Society and was knighted by the Queen of England.

Caging the Guest

Jean-Marie Lehn (1939-)
— *French chemist* —

Even before he won his Nobel Prize, **Jean-Marie Lehn**'s reputation for brilliance and uncanny insight was attracting disciples from all over the world. His Nobel work gave scientists a key to the thousands of chemical reactions that go on in our bodies. Somehow the right chemicals seem to react at just the right places.

When a chemical comes to "visit" a site, if it's the right one, something happens. The "host" captures the visitor in a "cage," much as a key fits into a specially prepared lock. Lehn built such a cage. This inspired other researchers to build their own cages to study different biochemical reactions. Now, because of the work of Jean-Marie Lehn, our understanding of how body chemicals fit together and "talk" to each other is growing explosively.

John Muir and John Burroughs

Defender of the Wilderness

John Muir (1838-1914)
— Scottish-American naturalist & conservationist —
    John Muir's laboratory was the whole world. In walking

trips in the United States and Canada, as well as nearly all the other continents, he observed and studied our planet's natural wonders. His detailed journals provided material for eloquent and inspiring books and articles that helped to build public interest in nature. Fighting powerful business interests that wanted to exploit the natural resources of wilderness areas, Muir stirred up support for conservation. He helped to win National Park status for the Yosemite and Sequoia regions of California and to defend them from developers.

Think of a Delicious Meal

Ivan Pavlov (1849-1936)
— *Russian physiologist* —

When you *think* of a delicious meal, things begin to happen. Your mouth salivates; your stomach juices begin to flow. **Ivan Pavlov,** the great Russian physiologist, coined the term "conditioned reflex" to describe such reactions. Although Pavlov used dogs in most of his experiments, his findings apply to human beings, too. Pavlov became so revered in Russia that he was just about the only Russian who could criticize the Soviet authorities during the trying decades of the 1920s and 30s and get away with it. "For the kind of social experiment that you are making, I would not sacrifice a frog's hind legs!" All they did in response to this remark was to name a major medical institute after him.

First Polio, Next AIDS?

Jonas Salk (1914-)
— *American physician and researcher* —

Jonas Salk is world famous for developing the Salk vaccine against polio. Thanks to his efforts, this frightening and deadly disease is virtually extinct in this country and in most others where Salk's vaccine (or a subsequent one, the Sabin vaccine) is used widely. Most recently, Salk has turned his attention to developing a safe and effective vaccine against AIDS.

If he succeeds in developing a safe and effective vaccine against AIDS, he will be ranked among the great medical pioneers of all time.

Explaining Your Behavior

John B(roadus) Watson (1878-1958)
— American psychologist —

Why are some people afraid of the dark, of heights, or of cats? Behavioral patterns like these and many others can be explained by several different psychological theories. One is called *behaviorism,* which explores the relationship between external events (stimuli) and human behavior. **John B. Watson,** a pioneer in this field of psychology, is often called the "Father of Behaviorism." Although this explanation of human and even animal behavior is still quite controversial, today behaviorism has a strong following in the scientific community.

CHAPTER 12

JOHN IN SPORTS

The Most Durable Catcher

Johnny Bench (Johnny Lee Bench) (1947-)
— American baseball catcher —

Johnny Bench was easily the best catcher in the league while he played baseball. And yet in the first major league free agent draft in 1965, seven other catchers were chosen before him! He showed them, though — he was named Rookie of the Year in 1967. Bench played seventeen seasons in the majors and won the Golden Glove award in ten of those. He proved his durability by catching 100 or more games thirteen years in a row, which tied a record. But he was much more than a defensive player. Johnny Bench led the league in home runs two years, and in RBIs three years. All together, he hit 327 home runs, the most for any catcher, ever.

Changing Sides

Jocko Conlan (John Bertrand Conlan) (1899-1989)
— American baseball umpire —

Outfielder **Jocko Conlan** of the Chicago White Sox was sidelined with an injury in the summer of 1935, when he was called on to pinch hit — for an umpire who had collapsed in the 114 degree heat. Conlan took his new role seriously: He was soon involved in a rhubarb with his own manager when he called teammate Luke Appling out on a close play. Jocko Conlan was a major-league out-fielder for just two seasons, but in 1941 he came back to the majors as a full-time umpire. This second baseball career lasted twenty-five years, and Conlan was one of the very few umpires ever elected to baseball's Hall of Fame.

Down for the Count

Jack Dempsey (William Harrison Dempsey) (1895-1983)
— American boxer —

One of the most memorable moments in sports was the famous "Long Count." It happened in a rematch between **Jack Dempsey** and Gene Tunney for the heavyweight boxing championship of the world. Tunney had dethroned Dempsey, the long-reigning former champion, the year before. But Dempsey had been out of shape. Now he would show this young upstart. He did. He knocked Tunney down decisively. As he stood over the fallen champ, the referee motioned Dempsey to a neutral corner. Dempsey refused to move. The referee motioned again, but Dempsey stood firm. A third time the referee gestured. Five or six seconds had gone by — an eternity in boxing — and the knockdown count had not begun yet! Finally, Dempsey moved to a neutral corner. At the count of nine, a groggy Tunney struggled to his feet. Eventually he recovered and defeated Dempsey, ending a great career in boxing.

A Risky Sport

Jean-Claude Killy (1943-)
— French skier —

"I take all the risks." That's what **Jean-Claude Killy** said, and he had the broken bones to prove it. But apparently the risks were worth it. For the rest of his life he will be remembered as the French skier who won three gold medals in the 1968 Olympics. Not only did it make him a millionaire with a flood of endorsements and other financial opportunities, but it made him an international hero. In France, it put him in a class by himself,

Jean-Claude Killy

revered and idolized by the masses. It was impossible for him to walk down the street without being recognized by dozens of passersby. Even today, long after his historic feats on the slopes, he carries clout. It was largely through his efforts that the 1992 Winter Olympics will be held in France.

Bad Luck Couldn't Stop This Champ

Jack Kramer (John Albert Kramer) (1921-)
— American tennis player, promoter —

As a boy, **Jack Kramer** loved football, but after he broke a rib his parents made him take up tennis. He liked tennis even more. He played hard and rose quickly to the top, becoming the boys' National champ. At eighteen he was one of the youngest representatives on the U.S. Davis Cup team, but the next year he missed the Nationals because of appendicitis. When he was twenty, food poisoning kept him from winning the final match in the Nationals. Then Kramer served in the Coast Guard during World

War II, and his tennis competition came to a complete halt. In 1946 he finally won the U.S. Nationals, and the next year he won at Wimbledon before he turned pro. In 1968 Jack Kramer received the highest honor a player can achieve — he was named to the International Tennis Hall of Fame.

Ivan Lendl

Number One

Ivan Lendl (1960-)
— Czech tennis player —

As far back as he can remember, **Ivan Lendl** has been "slugging it out" on the tennis court. As a toddler, he would tag along to the court with his parents, who were both ranked players in Czechoslovakia. After a successful junior career, Lendl turned pro in 1978. But it was not until 1984 that he was able to break through and win his first Grand Slam event, the French Open, against John McEnroe. Since then, Ivan has put together one of the most impressive stretches in Open Tennis History — three U.S.

Opens, two French Opens, one Australian Open title, and an additional thirty-two tournament titles. Ivan Lendl has been ranked #1 in the world five times, holds seven Grand Slam titles and has amassed the world's record in career earnings.

The Mellowing of McEnroe

John McEnroe (John Patrick McEnroe, Jr.) (1959-)
— American tennis player —

Few athletes were as colorful as **John McEnroe** in his rise to the top of tennis, but his sizzling serves were rivaled by his explosive temper. The press called him loudmouthed, and crowds loved to boo him wherever he went. No one could deny McEnroe's talent, though — he won four U.S. open singles titles and was a three-time winner at Wimbledon,. In the late 1980s McEnroe returned to tennis a changed man: even tempered, but still competitive. His change in attitude occurred with his marriage to movie star Tatum O'Neal, and the birth of their son.

Jack Nicklaus

Dominant Golden Bear

Jack Nicklaus (Jack William Nicklaus) (1940-)
— American golfer, entrepreneur —

Few athletes have dominated a sport as has **Jack Nicklaus.** During a span of almost thirty years, this distinctive figure won twenty major tournaments and many lesser ones. No one has equaled that record, and with the increased pace of competition, it is unlikely that anyone ever will. Still active in golf, Nicklaus also heads a golf course design business. In 1988 he was named "Golfer of the Century" by a panel of golfing officials and journalists.

First Black Major Leaguer

Jackie Robinson (John Roosevelt Robinson) (1919-1972)
— American baseball player —

He was chosen specially for the job. He was told he would be insulted every day — many times a day. But he had to turn the other cheek, and hide his explosive anger. His friends would say he sold out. He might lose respect. Did he still want the job? Yes! And **Jackie Robinson,** the first black baseball player in the major leagues, gave a magnificent performance — on the field, in the clubhouse, and just about anywhere he went. He won the hearts of fans everywhere and picked up the Rookie of the Year honors along the way. His lifetime .311 batting average and his brilliant fielding record made him an automatic first round choice for the baseball Hall of Fame.

Three-Time World Champion

Jackie Stewart (John Young Stewart) (1939-)
— Scottish race driver —

Jackie Stewart watched more friends die racing cars than many soldiers do during war time. In all, while he was driving over a period of twelve years, twelve good friends were smashed to death. Finally, after winning his third world championship race, Jackie called it quits. He had made the decision months before he quit, but he hadn't told his wife. He knew what it would be like for her to make the life/death countdown: just six more races to go, then five . . . What if he were killed with four races to go, or two, or in his last race? At last it was all over. Stewart stopped racing after 1973, but he still appears on TV and radio as a world-recognized authority on the motor industry.

Mr. Quarterback

Johnny Unitas (John Constantine Unitas) (1933-)
— American football quarterback, restauranteur —

In commemoration of the National Football League's fiftieth anniversary, **Johnny Unitas** was voted the greatest quarterback of all time. The irony is that Unitas was rejected, first by virtually all of the college football teams he applied to (he was too small, they said) and then by the Pittsburgh Steelers, who dropped him before the season began. Only a chance letter by a fan to the coach of the Baltimore Colts resulted in a tryout and a signing. Then, in his first game as quarterback, Unitas had his first pass intercepted for a touchdown. Before the season was over, though, he led the Colts to four victories in the remaining games. From there he went on to superstardom.

Tarzan Was a Swimming Star

Johnny Weissmuller (Peter John Weissmuller) (1904-1984)
— American swimmer, movie actor —

Johnny Weissmuller wasn't just Tarzan in the movies; he was a kind of real-life hero, too. For ten years he dominated the swimming scene. Once a sickly child who had been prescribed swimming as therapy, he had found his element. For a decade he raced in everything from fifty yards up to half a mile, and no one in the entire world could beat him. Weissmuller won five gold medals in the Olympics and set sixty-seven world swimming records. He was a natural for the Tarzan movies and played in twelve films until he was too old for the part. Then he played Jungle Jim in movies and on TV.

CHAPTER 13

JOHN
WORLD LEADERS

John Adams

Our Second President

John Adams *(1735-1826)*
— 2nd U.S. President —
    John Adams is called the Father of American Independ-

ence because of the great role he played in helping the colonies gain their independence from Britain. In the first presidential election of the new nation, he received the second highest number of electoral votes and became the first vice president of the United States. In the 1796 election he edged out Thomas Jefferson by three electoral votes and became our second president. In one of history's most astonishing coincidences, John Adams and Thomas Jefferson both died on July 4th — exactly fifty years after they signed the Declaration of Independence.

Silent Cal

(John) Calvin Coolidge (1872-1933)
— 30th U.S. President —

John Calvin Coolidge was a quiet man, who chose his words carefully, but when he spoke people stopped to listen. His stand against striking policemen when he was governor of Massachusetts captured the nation's attention: "There is no right to strike against the public safety by anybody, anywhere, any time." Although Coolidge was a popular president who would surely have won a third term in office if family tragedies hadn't prompted him to retire, he is said to have greatly contributed to the stock market crash and Great Depression with his laissez-faire presidential policies.

Ivan the Terrible

Ivan IV of Russia (1530-1584)
— First Czar of Russia —

Ivan IV became the leader of Russia at the age of three, but he was a pawn in the hands of noblemen who mistreated him and really controlled the country. At sixteen, Ivan declared himself Russia's first Czar, or Emperor, and greatly limited the power of the noblemen. Although he had a terrible temper, Ivan's first years as a ruler were impressive. He instituted reforms that gave the people more say in the government, opened trade between Russia and England, and began to expand the Russian borders. But after the death of his beloved wife, Anastasya, Ivan's temper grew uncontrollable. He began persecuting his subjects for trivial things and mercilessly slaughtered thousands; he even killed his own beloved son in a fit of rage. This violent temper brought grief to the Czar and his land, and he is remembered by the well earned sobriquet, Ivan the Terrible.

Grantor of the Magna Carta

John Lackland (1167-1216)
— *King of England* —

Considering how popular the name John has always been in England, it's surprising that there has been only one English **King John.** He was the youngest son of King Henry II, and by the time Henry had given his other three sons portions of Britain, there was nothing left for John. The young prince was then known as "Lackland." John Lackland spent a good deal of his life involved in schemes and plots to gain power from his father and brothers and ultimately became King of England. He was a good administrator, but the most notable achievement of his reign was actually yielded with great reluctance. King John signed the Magna Carta, which for the first time put into writing the rights and privileges of the common people.

A Fascist King?

Juan Carlos I (Juan Carlos Alfonso Victor Maria de Borbon y Borbon) (1938-)
— *King of Spain* —

Juan Carlos learned from his father's mistake. Don Juan, Juan Carlos' father, was a direct descendant of Spanish royalty, and he wanted to be King of Spain. At the time, Spain was ruled by the military fascist dictator, Franco. Don Juan's outspoken opposition caused his family to be exiled, but later Franco decided to groom Juan Carlos to be his successor. The young prince obligingly agreed with all that Franco taught him, and when the dictator died he was sure the new ruler would continue his fascist policies. But Juan Carlos had only been pretending agreement; when he became King in 1975, he surprised the world by establishing a democratic government in Spain.

John F. Kennedy

King Jack of Camelot

John Fitzgerald Kennedy (1917-1963)
— 35th U.S. President —

    John F. Kennedy was an extremely popular president. His style and charm were reminiscent of the days of King Arthur and the Knights of the Round Table. Some criticize his domestic and international policies, but others remember how he safely brought the country through several world crises involving Berlin, Cuba, and Russia. They remember how he negotiated important nuclear arms concessions, created a nationwide excitement over achievements in space, fought for equal rights for blacks, instituted food stamps for the poor, and helped form the Peace Corps. Most people who are old enough to remember the year 1963 can recall exactly where they were when they heard the news that President Kennedy had been shot by an assassin, ending the life of one of America's most colorful leaders.

Dictator for the Masses

Juan Domingo Peron (1895-1974)
— *Dictator of Argentina* —

Eva Duarte, or Evita as she was better known, helped her lover **Juan Peron** to rise from prisoner to President of Argentina. The two were married and ruled together with an iron hand. Although the working class was granted many privileges they did not have before, freedom of speech and other freedoms were greatly restricted under the rule of the Perons. After nearly ten years in power, Peron was ousted in a revolutionary coup and fled the country. Eighteen years later he was invited back and re-elected as Argentina's president. He might have enjoyed many more years as leader, if he had not died in office one year later.

Rebel Turned Friend

Jan Christian Smuts (1870-1950)
— *Prime Minister of South Africa* —

Sometimes it can be hard to decide just where our loyalties lie. Such was the case for **Jan Christian Smuts.** Born in what is now South Africa, of Dutch heritage, he was educated in England and had strong ties to the British. When the Boer War broke out between the British and the Dutch (Boers), Smuts served in the

Boer Army as General. Although the British won the war, Smuts had a lot of influence with the victors. He was largely instrumental in the uniting of various South African colonies into the Union of South Africa. During World War I, Smuts helped form the League of Nations, and in 1919 he became South Africa's prime minister, serving until he was defeated in 1924. At the outbreak of World War II he again became prime minister. He overruled the general consensus and joined with the Allies. After the war he helped set up the United Nations.

CHAPTER 14

JOHN AS A LAST NAME

All the Johns we have talked about so far share the same first name, in its numerous variations used around the world. But there is another group of people who might also be considered part of the vast John Clan: those whose *last* names are variations of John.

Actually, surnames came to be used in the first place mainly because of common names like John. At any one time, up to a third of all the males in a particular English village might have been named John. Last names made it easier to tell which one of them was being referred to. A common way of forming a surname was to specify the person's father. So present-day names like Johnson, Jackson, Jensen, and Hanson, as well as Janowicz and Ivanov, simply mean "John's son." The number of surnames stemming from variations of John is very large, and some of them — such as Jones and Johnson — are among the most common of all last names.

The Famous Signature

John Hancock (1737-1793)
— American merchant, official, and Revolutionary leader —
John Hancock is the most famous signer of the Declaration of Independence, because he was the first, and because his

John Hancock

signature is the biggest. Today, his name is synonymous with the entire concept of a signature. John Hancock did much more than sign America's most important document, however. He was the first governor of the state of Massachusetts and served nine terms before he died in office. He was also president of the Continental Congress. His one regret was that he was not chosen as commander-in-chief of the Revolutionary forces — he lost that position to George Washington.

The First President of the United States

John Hanson *(1721-1783)*
— American Revolutionary War leader —
George Washington was America's first elected President,

103

right? Actually, **John Hanson,** Maryland's Continental Congress representative, was elected by the Continental Congress as "President of the United States in Congress Assembled" in 1781 —George Washington became the nation's "first president" eight years later! But Hanson only presided over Congress, and did not have any of the powers that the Constitution gave to the President of the United States of America. Two-hundred years later, George Washington is remembered as the "Father of our country," and John Hanson — the president of the nation's first government — is a forgotten footnote in history.

Charismatic Black Leader

Jesse Louis Jackson (1941-)
— American civil rights leader, politician, clergyman —
Talented **Jesse Jackson** could have been a big-league baseball player, but he turned down the Chicago White Sox' offer to graduate from college with honors instead. He had his sights set higher. His success in winning more jobs and better services for blacks in Chicago through Operation Breadbasket and Operation PUSH and his flair for attracting media coverage soon made him a national figure. In the 1984 and 1988 Democratic primaries he emerged as a serious presidential candidate, and he had an important input into the Democratic Platform developed at the 1988 Convention in Atlanta, Georgia. Jesse Jackson may yet one day become the first black president of the United States.

Gentleman Jackson

John Jackson (1769-1845)
— British pugilist —
John Jackson won the boxing Championship of England in 1795. He was responsible for helping make boxing a legitimate British sport. Although he reigned as champion for eight years, he made only three public appearances in the ring. When the undefeated champ retired he opened a school of self-defense. "Gen-

104

tleman" Jackson's teachings instituted the scientific principles of boxing, which included fancy footwork and countering blows. Many young aristocrats, like the poet, Lord Byron, joined his school to learn the nation's new sport.

Mr. October

Reggie (Reginald Martinez) Jackson (1946-)
— American baseball player —

In the late 1970s **Reggie Jackson** was one of baseball's biggest and most colorful stars — on and off the field. He is one of the greatest home run hitters of all time, with 563 to his credit. The peak of his career came in the deciding game of the 1977 World Series when he drove in five runs with three consecutive home runs. The very next year he hit two home runs in the World Series. Reggie will become eligible for the baseball Hall of Fame in 1992, and there is no doubt in anyone's mind that he will be elected on the very first ballot.

Electric John

Elton John (Reginald Kenneth Dwight) (1947-)
— British singer, musician, composer —

Elton John loves to put on a show. He is famous not only for his music but also for his crazy fashions and impulsive stage performances. Born as Reginald Dwight, he was playing classical pieces on the piano by the time he was four years old. Elton met poet Bernie Taupin through a newspaper ad, and together they have created some of the best loved music of the 1970s and 80s.

Contemporary Art Leader

Jasper Johns (1930-)
— American artist —

Jasper Johns' art defies labels, yet the critics still use them. He's not pop, commercial, abstract, impressionist, or Cubist, nor does his art deal with social issues. For the most part, Johns is a self-taught artist. During his early years in New York, he was awarded a scholarship for commercial art school with the explanation that the grant was based on financial need rather than merit in his work. Unwilling to accept assistance on those terms, he left the art school after two semesters. Eventually, he was able to support himself doing free-lance window display work, while he pursued his ambition to be an artist. Represented in museums and private collections around the world, Johns is one of the most renowned artists today, producing paintings, drawings, prints, and sculpture with a masterful technique.

The Strange Johnson Coincidence

Andrew Johnson (1808-1875)/Lyndon Baines Johnson 1908-1973)
— 17th and 36th Presidents of the United States —

One of the great coincidences in history involves America's two Presidents named Johnson. Both **Andrew** and **Lyndon Johnson** became president after their predecessor was assassinated. They both came from the South, and each had two daughters. They both have six letters in their first names, they were the only two vice presidents to have kidney stones, and they were born exactly one hundred years apart. There are many other factors concerning the two Johnsons and the Presidents they served that add to the uncanny coincidences of the their lives.

Grand Slam Jones

Bobby Jones (Robert Tyre Jones) (1902-1971)
— American amateur golfer —

Bobby Jones was a lawyer, but he is remembered as one of the greatest golfers of all time. He is the only man ever to win the four golf events of his time, the US Open, British Open, US Amateur and British Amateur tournaments. He achieved this Grand Slam victory in 1930, and he retired from golf that year at the age of twenty-eight. In 1934 Bobby Jones helped form the Masters Tournament, which is now one of today's four main competitions in golf.

The Record Breaker

Jesse Owens (James Cleveland Owens) (1913-1980)
— American track and field athlete —

    In the 1936 Berlin Olympics, Adolf Hitler walked out of the games in dismay. American black athlete **Jesse Owens** had won four gold medals — quite a blow to the German host who claimed the superiority of the Aryan race. Though all of his records have been broken over the years, no track athlete has ever been able to rival Jesse Owens' long list of record-breaking performances.

CHAPTER 15

CURIOSITIES AND MEMORABLE MOMENTS

Pilgrim Love Triangle

Back in 1621, Captain Miles Standish of the Plymouth settlement had his eye on pretty Priscilla Mullens. The captain, a gruff soldier type, figured that his young roommate, **John Alden,** could do a smoother job of proposing to Priscilla on his behalf. John wasn't very enthusiastic about that idea — he was in love with Priscilla, too. But he did the favor for his friend, only to be chided by the Pilgrim maiden, "Why don't you speak for yourself, John?" Eventually, he did. They married and had eleven children. One of their descendants, **John Quincy Adams,** became a United States President. Another, Henry Wadsworth Longfellow, immortalized their story in his narrative poem, *The Courtship of Miles Standish.*

When Dreams Come True

Dreams sometimes have the most uncanny way of unlocking hidden mysteries. **(Jean) Louis Agassiz** had already built quite a reputation as a world-renowned fossil fish expert when he came across a fossil of an unidentified fish species that had lived millions of years in the past. The fossil was embedded in rock and in such bad condition that he couldn't make out the details. That night Agassiz dreamed he saw the fish alive, swimming contentedly in the water. He had the same dream two more nights in a

Jean-Louis Agassiz

row. On the third night he kept a pencil by his bed, and when he awoke he quickly sketched down the fine details. Using the sketch as a guide, Agassiz began to chisel away more of the rock enclosing the fossil. A thin layer of rock broke away and revealed the fish — and the fine details corresponded exactly to his sketch.

The Richest Man in America

John Jacob Astor was the richest man in America in the mid-nineteenth century. He had well over 25 million dollars — a sum worth many, many times that value in today's market. When

John Jacob Astor

someone has that much money, his perception of the worth of a dollar is quite different from that of the average person. Astor once remarked, "A man who has a million dollars is as well off as if he were rich."

Coffee Fiends

Are you one of those people who don't feel really human until you have your cup of coffee in the morning? Composer **Johann Sebastian Bach** poked fun at that all-too-common type back in the eighteenth century, in a one-act operetta called the *Coffee Cantata*. "Dear Father, don't be so strict," was the musical plea when a father chided his daughter about her coffee habit. "If I can't have my little demitasse of coffee three times a day, I'm just a dried-up piece of roast goat!"

Another prominent eighteenth-century figure, philosopher **Jean-Jacques Rousseau,** was a coffee addict too. (Could there be some relationship between caffeine and the Enlightenment?) Rousseau drank so much coffee, it was said, that when he died, "he just missed doing it with a cup of coffee in his hand."

The Biggest Painting — Ever!

John Banvard never amounted to much, but he certainly left behind a monumental bit of himself when he died: a painting twelve feet high and three miles long! He began his enormous project in 1841, as he traveled along the Mississippi. The entire work, which he called the "Panorama," was wrapped around two huge spindles and slowly unrolled. Every day hundreds of paying customers watched the scenery of the Mississippi scroll by in a two-hour show. Banvard toured the nation, and England, too. Both President Polk and Queen Victoria expressed their approval after viewing this unusual work of art. Before it was all over, Banvard netted over $200,000, an impressive sum in the nineteenth century. Today, the "Panorama" is not found in the Smithsonian or anywhere else. After Banvard's death, it was cut to pieces, and individual scenes were used as backdrops in various theatres.

Generous Jack

On radio and television, comedian **Jack Benny** was noted for his miserly ways. A typical skit portrayed him confronted by a mugger:

Mugger: "Your money or your life!"

Benny: (long pause) "I'm thinking, I'm thinking."

The real Jack Benny was quite different, giving generously of his time and talents in fund-raising benefit shows. He was also a devoted husband to his on-stage "girlfriend," Mary Livingstone.

His will provided that after his death Mary would receive a single long-stemmed rose every day for the rest of her life.

The Great Carsoni

Johnny Carson, America's favorite talk show host, started his show-biz career at fourteen with a magic act called "The Great Carsoni." From his Norfolk, Nebraska beginnings he went on to radio and local L.A. TV. His big break came when he filled in for Red Skelton with a comedy monologue. "The kid is great, just great," exclaimed Jack Benny. It wasn't long before Johnny had his own network show, launching a career that has won him six Emmy Awards.

Betrayed by the "Lady in Red"

John Dillinger robbed more banks in a year than Jesse James did in his sixteen-year career. He was also a killer, and yet to most of America he was a hero. Longtime Public Enemy Number One, Dillinger was legendary for his daring and ingenious escapes from the law. Once he bluffed his way out of an Indiana prison with a gun he carved out of wood with a razor and stained with shoe polish. Eventually, Dillinger's luck ran out. A friend, Anna Sage, was forced to make a deal with the FBI. She informed them that Dillinger, who had recently undergone plastic surgery, was going to be at the Biograph Theatre in Chicago accompanied by "The Lady in Red." As Dillinger was leaving the theatre, he was surrounded by lawmen and shot to death. But some say that Dillinger outsmarted the law once again — he knew about the FBI plan and it was a different man who was shot. Whatever the truth really is, he was never heard from again.

She Had The Last Laugh

Poet **John Dryden** once wrote cynically, "all heiresses are beautiful." He neglected to take his own implied advice, and his marriage was not a happy one, although his wife bore him three

sons. He penned an epitaph, intended for his wife:
"Here lies my wife: here let her lie!
Now she's at rest, and so am I."
Alas for Dryden, his wife outlived him.

Overbudget

In making a movie one can always be sure of two things:
The movie is going to run overtime and overbudget. Director **John Ford,** noted for his gruff manner and practical approach, had his own way of dealing with such problems. When producer Samuel Goldwyn came onto the set to inform Ford that the shooting schedule was one day behind, the director was unworried. "Sam," he asked, "about how many script pages do you think I should shoot a day?" Caught by surprise, Goldwyn thought a minute, then shrugged, "I don't know . . . about five." Without a word, Ford picked up a copy of the script and forcibly ripped out five pages. "Okay, Sam," he said calmly, "now we're right on schedule."

What a Man!

When Napoleon and **Johann Goethe** met, both men were impressed. Goethe saw Napoleon as a great liberator. Before they met, Napoleon had read Goethe's novel, *The Sorrows of Young Werther,* seven times. Napoleon's comment on first seeing the great writer was "Voilà un homme!" ("There is a man!")

Straight from the President's Mouth

George Washington rarely smiled. It wasn't that he had no sense of humor; he was just self-conscious about his teeth — they weren't his. In fact, his false teeth were made of wood, which picked up all sorts of foul odors. Worse still, they never fit him very well. The man responsible for these unfortunate effects was **John Greenwald,** the President's dentist.

He Died With His Boots Off

Gunslingers of the Old West often expected to live up to the old maxim and die in a gun fight. **John Henry Holliday,** or Doc Holliday as he was known, was always sure this was how he would go. Instead, he died of tuberculosis. When he awoke from a coma, he realized his fate, drank a shot of whiskey, and sighed, "This is funny!" before he died.

A Traitor Turned Hero

During the Revolutionary war, being a supporter of the British in the American colonies was a risky position to take. Aside from the hateful glances and constant insults, personal mayhem was not uncommon. So Dr. **John Jeffries** was forced to give up his formerly successful medical practice and flee to England. There he met Jean-Pierre Blanchard, the balloonist, and discovered a new passion. He took up ballooning and collaborated with Blanchard in the first successful balloon crossing of the English channel in 1785. Jeffries eventually returned to America, his Tory sympathies during the war forgiven in the glow of his celebrity as an intrepid balloonist.

Hero of the High Seas

John Paul Jones is America's favorite Naval hero. School children all across the country are taught about the great moment in history when Jones' ship, Le Bonhomme Richard, was confronted by the commander of the British ship, the Serapis. John Paul Jones was ordered to surrender, and although his ship was badly damaged he declared courageously, "I have not yet begun to fight." Actually, John Paul Jones never really claimed to have said those memorable words. "I answered him in the most determined negative," was the way he described the incident. The Bonhomme Richard eventually sank, but Jones and his men captured the British ship and went down in history.

114

John Paul Jones

Number One Job in the Country

Shortly after he was elected president, **John F. Kennedy** was asked how he liked his new job. Kennedy replied: "The pay is good and I can walk to work."

The Longest Beard

Some people will go to extraordinary lengths to prove a point. Others will suffer great inconvenience just to be able to say "I'm number one!" **Hans Langseth,** a Norwegian who emigrated to the United States in 1912, must have wished many times that he hadn't begun his lifelong project. A beard measuring 17 feet 6 inches can be a nuisance. But it has probably assured him a permanent footnote in history, for the longest beard ever grown by a man. Langseth died in 1927, but his beard can be seen at the Smithsonian Institution.

Never Argue With A Woman

The Irish scholar **Sir John Mahaffy** was once involved in a discussion with a feminist. She stated her case succinctly. She was a woman, he was a man, so what was the difference between the two of them? Sir John replied: "Madam, I can't conceive."

Dominican Export

Pitcher **Juan Marichal** was spotted by a Giants' scout in his native Dominican Republic, where baseball fever runs high and major league ballplayers are a major export. When Marichal joined the Giants' farm club in Michigan City, Indiana, in 1958, he spoke only Spanish — which could be a bit of a handicap in Middle America. He wound up having a ham sandwich and apple pie for every meal during his first week with the team, explaining later that he had seen someone order that at the diner the first day, and it was the only thing he knew how to ask for. Eventually Marichal learned English, but he never had any trouble making himself understood on the baseball field. Over a period of sixteen years with the Giants, he won twenty or more games in six separate seasons, and one of his many wins was a no-hitter.

Only When it Rains

John Marshall was probably the greatest Chief Justice of the Supreme Court in U.S. history. But he and his colleagues had gained a reputation for having a bit too much to drink while pursuing their judicial business. So they resolved to drink only when it rained.

John Marshall

During one of their weekly consultation days, Marshall asked one of the justices, Joseph Story, to go to the window to see if it was raining. Story regretfully reported back, "No, Mr. Chief Justice, there isn't the slightest sign of rain." That didn't daunt John Marshall, noted for his brilliantly reasoned decisions. "Justice Story," he answered sternly, "I think that is the shallowest and most illogical opinion I have ever heard you deliver; you forget that our jurisdiction is as broad as the Republic, and by the laws of nature it must be raining some place in our jurisdiction. Waiter, bring on the rum."

The Bargain of the Century

In what must surely rank as one of the shrewdest deals in

117

publishing history, London publisher Samuel Simmons bought the copyright of *Paradise Lost* from **John Milton** in 1667 for the sum of five pounds, plus an additional five pounds to be paid for each of three subsequent editions. Milton lived to collect only ten pounds for the greatest epic poem in the English language. After his death, his widow Elizabeth sold the remaining rights to Simmons for eight pounds.

A Name Like "Sandwich"?

Can you imagine having a name like "Sandwich"? Of course, if the word hadn't been invented yet, it wouldn't be so bad. Indeed, the word comes from Lord Sandwich, the title of **John Montagu,** the fourth earl of Sandwich and the British first lord of the Admiralty during the American Revolution. A compulsive gambler, he would never leave the gambling table while he had a hot streak going — not even to get something to eat. Instead, he had a servant fetch him a slice of meat or cheese, nestled between two pieces of bread. He became famous for this gustatory innovation, especially after one notorious game in 1762, when he gambled nonstop for twenty-four hours, eating sandwiches with one hand while he held his cards with the other.

Sharp Trader

Financier and art collector **John Pierpont Morgan, Sr.** was noted for his shrewdness in business matters. Once budding art dealer Joseph Duveen made the mistake of underestimating him. He brought Morgan a selection of thirty miniatures. Six of them were real prizes; the others were rather ordinary. The financier looked them over and then asked, "How much do you want for the lot?" Eagerly, Duveen gave him a price for the collection, figuring in much higher amounts for the six valuable ones. "I'll take six," Morgan informed him and then unerringly picked out the six best. Dividing Duveen's price by thirty and multiplying by six, he handed over the sum — far less than the miniatures were worth.

"You're only a boy, Joe," said Duveen's uncle Henry, who had previously been handling the Morgan account. "It takes a man to deal with Morgan."

The King Is Always Right

Sir John Pringle was a noted Scottish physician in the late 1700s. During the reign of King George III, Pringle presided as President of the Royal Society — the oldest scientific organization in the world. Quite suddenly Pringle resigned from the position. The announced explanation for his resignation was that he was not in good health. However, another story provides quite a different perspective. King George III had informed Pringle that Benjamin Franklin's lightning rods were all wrong. The ends of the lightning rods should be pointed, not blunt as Franklin asserted. Pringle's retort was probably what really cost him his job: "The laws of nature are not changeable at royal pleasure."

South Carolina Under the French

Parlez-vous français? You might if fate hadn't changed history. **Jean Ribaut** and his three French ships landed in Florida in 1562. Ribaut claimed Florida for France, and headed north to settle what is now Port Royal, South Carolina. He named this first French colony in the New World, Charlesfort. Ribaut left the settlers and returned to France for fresh supplies and to bring back more Frenchmen to settle the colony. But France was in the midst of a religious war. Ribaut, a Protestant, had to flee to England and abandon all thought of helping his French comrades in America. Without new supplies, conditions at the settlement grew intolerable, and Charlesfort was abandoned. France lost a chance to gain a foothold on the American coast.

Money May Not Be Everything, But . . .

John D. Rockefeller was the first billionaire to celebrate

119

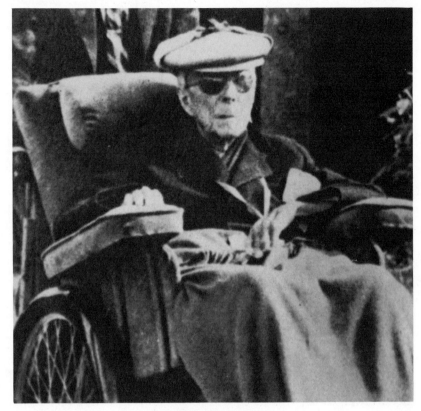

John D. Rockefeller

his ninetieth birthday. He lived to the ripe old age of ninety-eight. Later in his life he became quite a philanthropist and helped spread around a little of the giant fortune he had accumulated. However, at heart he remained the canny financier. At one birthday party his family presented him with an electric car to permit him to get around his estate more easily. "If it's all the same to you," he said, "I'd rather have the money."

In the Eye of the Beholder

Expatriate artist **John Singer Sargent** had built up an enviable reputation as a portrait painter in Paris when disaster struck. In 1884 he exhibited a portrait of a well-known Parisian beauty, Madame Pierre Gautreau. Sargent considered the painting his masterpiece, but critics found the low-cut dress and provocative pose too erotic. Rather tame by today's standards, the painting caused a scandal in nineteenth-century Paris. Sargent had to remove it from exhibition and retitled it *Madame X.* He was so notorious that he fled to London, which turned out to be a good career move. Within a few years, his portraits had become the rage of London. He even earned the luxury of being rude to his patrons when they tried his patience. To one woman who complained about her portrait, "The nose isn't right," Sargent suggested that she take it home and fix it up herself. Ultimately he painted more than four hundred portraits of wealthy notables, including two U.S. presidents, millionaires, and author Robert Louis Stevenson.

The American Rickshaw?

Picture the Orient, and one of the images that comes to mind is a Chinese coolie trotting along, pulling a rickshaw. This quintessentially Oriental mode of transportation was actually invented by an American. **Jonathan Scobie** was an American Baptist minister, serving in Yokohama, Japan in the 1860s. His wife was physically handicapped and so was doomed to remain home day after dreary day. Following an inspiration, Scobie constructed a two-wheel carriage — the rickshaw. When the residents of Yokohama saw Scobie's invention in operation, it was an instant hit and soon appeared all over Japan, and later in China.

The Monkey Trial

Today evolution is considered a scientific fact, but a recent poll of college students found that nearly 50% believe in creationism. The battle rages on more than a hundred years after Darwin, but never was this fight more apparent than in 1925 during the famous Monkey Trial. The world watched closely as a young science teacher, **John T. Scopes,** was tried for violating a Tennessee law requiring teachers to teach creationism. Scopes had refused. The court found him guilty and fined him one hundred dollars. The trial, however, was a real-life drama between world famous lawyers, William Jennings Bryant and Clarence Darrow, and was captured in the Hollywood movie, *Inherit the Wind.* Although the jury found Scopes guilty, the cause of academic freedom won a striking victory. Later, the verdict was overturned on a technicality: The fine was too high. The law was repealed by the Tennessee legislature in 1967.

Shh! The Master's Working

Sometimes living with a genius isn't easy. Finnish composer **Jean Sibelius** was often immersed in a flood of creative inspiration. His wife and children knew they had to be careful not to interrupt the flow of melodies in his mind. They tiptoed about, didn't speak to him in the morning until he broke the silence (indicating that he had descended to the world of ordinary mortals again), and never, *never* did they sing or whistle spontaneously. Even a workman painting the house had to be cautioned that his cheerful whistling was disturbing the Professor. Any stray tune could break his concentration, and the day's work was ruined. The family observed the rules respectfully and lovingly. Father was hard at work, and his art must come first.

Indian Princess

The story of **John Smith** and the beautiful Indian maiden, Pocahantas, is a treasured bit of American folklore. As Smith told it, he had been captured and sentenced to death by a hostile Indian tribe when Pocahantas, the chief's daughter, pleaded with her father to spare the handsome Englishman. When her pleas were unheeded, she bravely shielded Smith with her own body. At last, the chief relented, and Smith was released. Five years later, in 1613, the settlers kidnaped Pocahantas, hoping to use her as a hostage in negotiations with her father. She was treated courteously and fell in love with **John Rolfe,** one of the settlers. They were married after Pocahantas was converted to Christianity and baptized Lady Rebecca. In 1616, the couple sailed to England, where the fashionable nobility made quite a fuss over the Indian princess.

The Censoring of America

In the late 1930's **John Steinbeck**'s book, *The Grapes of Wrath,* was banned from many schools across the country. At the same time, it was also required reading at many other schools, such as Princeton and Harvard Universities. Steinbeck received many letters about his books. Some offered praise and encouragement over the controversy, but others came from angry people concerned with the harsh language he used. One letter contained the threat, "Beware. You will never get out of this world alive."

One Divorce Too Many

Johann Strauss may have been a genius when it came to music, but when it came to women he was a bit of a dunce. After he divorced his second wife, Angelika, he married for a third time. Angelika was furious. She was not going to let him off so easily. She made up an elaborate sign denouncing him and picketed his home. She paced back and forth, displaying the sign for all to see, and drew quite a sympathetic crowd.

The Magic Moment

What makes a prize-winning photograph? There's an element of luck — being at the right place at the right time — and an element of artistic skill. That magic mix of luck and skill that produces a Pulitzer-quality photo doesn't happen very often — perhaps only once in a lifetime. So it was for AP photographer **Jack Thornell,** who was the only photographer on the scene when a sniper's bullet cut down civil rights activist James Mere-

Jack Thornell

dith on a march for black voter registration near Hernando, Mississippi. He captured on film the instant of Meredith's fall and, peering out from the underbrush by the side of the road, a man who may have been the sniper. Thornell developed and printed the film himself and personally wired in the photo that captured a 1967 Pulitzer Prize.

Value

If you want to set an art dealer's heart racing, drop a hint of a previously undiscovered Vermeer. Paintings by the seventeenth-century Dutch artist **Jan Vermeer van Delft** are as scarce as they are valuable. The artist (who died in obscurity and poverty) lavished painstaking care on his paintings, with an almost photographic detail and an uncanny knack for using light to create a mood of tranquility. Only thirty or forty authentic Vermeers exist today, and there has been a lot of confusion about them. Often Vermeer didn't sign his paintings, and there were several other Jan Vermeers who also painted around the same period. To further muddy the issue, a 1940s Dutch artist named **Hans van Meegeren** made more than a million dollars forging Vermeers and selling them to museums and private collectors. When that story came out, it gave the real Vermeer's popularity an enormous boost.

Property of MGM

When Olympic swimming star **Johnny Weissmuller** signed with MGM to star in the *Tarzan* movies, the studio regarded him as a valuable property. No detail was overlooked, no matter how minor. Johnny's contract specified, for example, that his hair was never to be cut, only trimmed so that it grew long over his ears. Less minor details were attended to with equal efficiency: When Johnny's wife Bobbe opposed his movie career, the studio paid her a $10,000 bribe to leave him.

125

CHAPTER 16

NOTABLE QUOTES FROM NOTABLE JOHNS

Fred Allen (John F. Sullivan)
American comedian (1894-1956)

"A conference is a gathering of important people who singly can do nothing but together can decide that nothing can be done."

"I like long walks, especially when they are taken by people who annoy me."

"Television is a medium because well done is rare."

Jean Anouilh
French dramatist (1910-1987)

"I don't want people to love me. It makes for obligations."

"Every man thinks God is on his side."

John Arbuthnot
Scottish writer, physician (1667-1735)

"Law is a bottomless pit."

John Ashbery
American author (1927-)

"I don't want to read what is going to slide down easily; there has to be some crunch, a certain amount of resilience."

Johann Sebastian Bach
German composer (1685-1750)

"I was made to work; if you are equally industrious, you will be equally successful."

John Barrymore
American actor (1882-1942)

"In Genesis it says that it is not good for man to be alone, but sometimes it is a great relief."

"Sex is not taxed — but it can be taxing."

"You never realize how short a month is until you pay alimony."

John Barth
American writer (1930-)

"One must sometimes go forward by going back."

Jack Benny
American comedian (1894-1974)

"Age is strictly a case of mind over matter. If you don't mind, it doesn't matter."

Jean de la Bruyère
French writer (1645-1696)

"Life is a tragedy for those who feel, and a comedy for those who think."

"The best way to get on in the world is to make people believe it's to their advantage to help you."

"There are but three general events which happen to mankind: birth, life, and death. Of their birth they are insensible, they suffer when they die, and neglect to live."

127

John Bunyan
British writer, minister (1628-1688)

"Example is the school of mankind, and they will learn at no other."

John Burroughs
American naturalist (1837-1921)

"The Kingdom of Heaven is not a place, but a state of mind."

Johnny Carson
American comedian (1925-)

"Mail your packages early, so the post office can lose them in time for Christmas."

St. John Chrysostom
Greek religious leader (345(?)-407)

"Riches are not forbidden, but the pride of them is."

John Ciardi
American poet (1916-1986)

"Intelligence recognizes what has happened. Genius recognizes what will happen."

"Modern art is what happens when painters stop looking at girls and persuade themselves that they have a better idea."

Jean Cocteau
French writer/film maker (1891-1963)

"The instinct of nearly all societies is to lock up anybody who is truly free. First society begins by trying to beat you up. If this fails, they try to poison you. If this fails too, they finish by loading honors on your head."

"We must believe in luck. For how else can we explain the success of those we don't like."

John Jay Chapman
American writer (1862-1933)

"There are lots of people who can't think seriously without injuring their minds."

(John) Calvin Coolidge
30th American President (1872-1933)

"If you don't say anything, you won't be called on to repeat it."

"The business of America is business."

John E.E. Dalberg (Lord Acton)
British historian (1834-1902)

"The most certain test by which we judge whether a country is really free is the amount of security enjoyed by minorities."

Sir John Davies
British poet (1569-1626)

"Skill comes so slow, and life so fast doth fly,
"We learn so little and forget so much."

John Dewey
American educator (1859-1952)

"Anyone who has begun to think places some portion of the world in jeopardy."

John Dickinson
American statesman (1732-1808)

"Then join hand in hand, brave Americans all —
By uniting we stand, by dividing we fall."

John Erskine
American educator (1879-1951)

"Only if we can restrain ourselves is conversation possible. Good talk rises upon much discipline."

John Florio
British writer (1533-1625)

"Who will not suffer labor in this world, let him not be born."

Jean de la Fontaine
French fable writer (1621-1695)

"If you deal with a fox, think of his tricks."
"To hurry is useless. The thing to do is to set out in time."

John Ford
British writer (1586-1640(?))

"I am . . . a mushroom on whom the dew of heaven drops now and then."

John Kenneth Galbraith
American economist (1908-)

"Wealth is not without its advantages."

John Galsworthy
English writer (1867-1933)

"I shall pass through this world but once; any good things, therefore, that I can do, or any kindness that I can show to any human being, or dumb animal, let me do it now. Let me not deter it or neglect it, for I shall not pass this way again."

"One's eyes are what one is; one's mouth, what one becomes."

John Nance Garner
American Vice President (1868-1967)

"You have to do a little bragging on yourself even to your relatives — man doesn't get anywhere without advertising."

John Gay
English writer (1685-1732)

"I must have women. There is nothing unbends the mind like them."

"Praising all alike, is praising none."

J(ean) Paul Getty
American oil tycoon (1892-1976)

"If you get up early, work late, and pay your taxes, you will get ahead — if you strike oil."

"The weak shall inherit the earth — but not the mineral rights."

Johann Wolfgang von Goethe
German writer (1749-1832)

"Daring ideas are like chessmen moved forward; they may be beaten, but they may start a winning game."

"How people keep correcting us when we are young! There's always some bad habit or other they tell us we ought to get over. Yet most bad habits are tools to help us through life."

"If children grew up according to early indications, we should have nothing but geniuses."

"One ought, every day at least, to hear a little song, read a good poem, see a fine picture, and, if it were possible, to speak a few reasonable words."

"To measure up to all that is demanded of him, a man must over-estimate his capabilities."

"Unlike grownups, children have little need to deceive themselves."

John H. Holmes
American religious reformer (1879-1964)

"The universe is not hostile, nor yet is it friendly. It is simply indifferent."

John Huston
American director (1906-1987)

"I don't try to guess what a million people will like. It's hard enough to know what I like."

Ivan Illich
Austrian-American educator (1926-)

"In a consumer society there are inevitably two kinds of slaves; the prisoners of addiction and the prisoners of envy."

John Jensen
American educator (1911-)

"The trouble with life in the fast lane is that you get to the other end in an awful hurry."

John F. Kennedy
35th American president (1917-1963)

"Forgive your enemies, but never forget their names."
"Let us never negotiate out of fear. But let us never fear to negotiate."
"Victory has a hundred fathers, and defeat is an orphan."

John V. Lindsay
Former mayor of NYC (1921-)

"Not only is New York City the nation's melting pot, it is also the casserole, the chafing dish and the charcoal grill."

John Locke
British philosopher (1632-1704)

"It is one thing to show a man that he is in error, and another to put him in possession of the truth."

John Lydgate
British poet (c1370-1451)

"Love is more than gold or great riches."

John Marshall
U.S. Supreme Court Chief Justice (1755-1835)

"To listen well is as powerful a means of communication and influence as to talk well."

John Masefield
British poet laureate (1878-1967)

"Success is the brand on the brow of the man who has aimed too low."

Jackie Mason
American comedian (1931-)

"I have enough money to last me the rest of my life, unless I buy something."

John McEnroe
American tennis player (1959-)

"Everybody loves success, but they hate successful people."

Molière (Jean-Baptiste Poquelin)
French dramatist (1622-1673)

"A lover tries to stand in well with the pet dog of the house."

Jack Parr
American talk show host (1918-)

"I have never seen a bad television program, because I refuse to. God gave me a mind, and a wrist that turns things off."

Jean Renoir
French director (1894-1979)

"Is it possible to succeed without any act of betrayal?"

Jean Paul Richter
German writer (1763-1825)

"Passion makes the best observations and draws the most wretched conclusions."

John D. Rockefeller, Jr.
American philanthropist (1874-1960)

"The only question with wealth is what you do with it."

Jean-Jacques Rousseau
French philosopher (1712-1778)

"A person who can break wind is not dead."
"Man is born free; and everywhere he is in chains. One thinks himself the master of others, and still remains a greater slave than they."

John Ruskin
British writer/art critic (1819-1900)

"No human being, however great, or powerful, was ever so free as a fish."

"That country is the richest which nourishes the greatest number of noble and happy human beings."

"When a man is wrapped up in himself, he makes a pretty small package."

Jean-Paul Sartre
French philosopher (1905-1980)

"Three o'clock is always too late or too early for anything you want to do."

Johann Christoph Friedrich von Schiller
German poet (1759-1805)

"One can give advice comfortably from a safe port."

John Selden
British judge (1584-1654)

"Ignorance of the law excuses no man."

"'Tis not the drinking that is to be blamed, but the excess."

John Sheffield
First Duke of Buckingham (1684-1721)

"Learn to write well, or not to write at all."

Jean Sibelius
Finnish composer (1865-1957)

"Pay no attention to what critics say; no statue has ever been put up to a critic."

John Sloan
American artist (1871-1951)

"Consistency is the quality of a stagnant mind."

John Sterling
British writer (1806-1844)

"There is no lie that many men will not believe; there is no man who does not believe many lies; and there is no man who believes only lies."

Jonathan Swift
Irish satirist (1667-1745)

"May you live all the days of your life!"
"Promises and piecrust are made to be broken."

Sir John Vanbrugh
British architect (1664-1726)

"Thinking is to me the greatest fatigue in the world."

John Wilmot, *Earl of Rochester*
British poet (1647-1680)

"Before I got married I had six theories about bringing up children; now I have six children, and no theories."

CHAPTER 17

THE MANY NAMES OF JOHN

Roots of the John Clan

Today most people choose a name for their baby because they like the way it sounds, or perhaps to honor someone in the family or a person they liked or admired. But in ancient times, choosing a name for your child was a much more serious affair. Names were actually descriptions or dedications with very specific meanings. The name John comes from the Hebrew *Jehohanan* (pronounced "Yeh-ho-HAHN-ahn"), which was shortened to *Johanan* ("Yo-HAHN-anh"). The "Jeho-" root comes from "Jehovah," God, and Jehohanan means "God is gracious." Johanan can be found in the Old Testament, and it was a common Jewish name. It can be traced even further back to the Hebrew root *Chaanach*. (The "ch" in Hebrew has a guttural "kh' sound, not the "ch" in English words like "chair.") Channach is also the root of the feminine name Hannah, or Anne. The ancient Phoenicians apparently used these same masculine and feminine names.

How Names Change

Over the past 2000 years the original John roots have undergone many transformations. Dozens of cultures have adopted their own variations of the name, John. When people travel to other lands the spelling and pronunciation of a name is often modified to make it sound more familiar to the natives of the new home. That was how the old French Jehan became John as the Norman invaders were gradually absorbed into British culture. Sometimes a certain sound doesn't exist in a language, and a new sound replaces it. For example, Irish has no "j" sound, and John became Sean, or Shaun. But the Latin form Johannes passed directly into German without changing at all.

John Is a Popular Name

John was the most popular name for boys in all English-speaking countries from the sixteenth century until the 1950s. During the fifties, there were close to six million people named John in the United States alone. There are at least 100 variations of the name John in over thirty different languages, and in many countries the John-equivalent names have enjoyed a similar popularity over the years.

The John Clan

Here are some of the many names of John:

Ancas, Anno, Ans, Ansis, Anson, Ants, Enselis, Enskis, Eoghan, Eoin, Evan, Ewan, Ewen, Gian, Giankos, Giannakes, Giannes, Gianni, Giannini, Giannino, Gianozzo, Giavanni, Gioacchino, Giovanni, Giovanoli, Hanan, Hanas, Hanka, Hanneken, Hannes, Hanno, Hannus, Hans, Hanschen, Hansel, Hansl, Hansli, Hasli, Iaian, Iain, Ian, Ioannes, Ivan, Ivanjuschka, Jack, Jackie, Jackson, Jacky, Jan, Janek, Jani, Janis, Janke, Janko, Janne, Jannes, Jannik, Jano, Janos, Jantje, Jean, Jeanno, Jeannot, Jehan, Johohanan, Jen, Jenda, Jenkin, Jens, Jevin, Joanico, Joaninho, Joannes, Joannoulos, Joao, Joaozinho, Jock, Jocko, Jofa, Jofan, Johan, Johann, Johannes, John, Johhnie, Johnny, Johnston, Johny, Jon, Jonas, Jonatan, Jonathan, Jonathen, Jonathon, Jonathus, Jone, Jones, Joni, Jonothan, Jonothon, Jonkus, Jonkuttis, Jonnel, Jonny, Jonty, Jovan, Jovica, Juan, Juanity, Jveica, Jvic, Jvo, Nanni, Nannos, Owen, Sean, Seaghan, Seamas, Shan, Shane, Shaughn, Shaun, Shawn, Sion,

Vanechka, Vanja, Vanjucha, Vanjuschka, Vanka, Vanni, Yahya, Yanni, Yohanan, Zane

John Around The World

Here are some of the more common forms of the name John in different languages around the world:

Arabic: Yahya
Bavarian: Hansl, Johan
Belgian: Hanka, Hanneken, Hannes, Jan, Jehan
Bohemian: Jan
Czechoslavakian: Jan
Danish: Hans, Hanschen, Jan, Janne, Jantje, Jen, Jens, Johan
Dutch: Hans, Jan, Jantje, Johan, Johan, Johannes
English: Jack, Jacky, Jenkin, John, Johnny, Jonathan, Jonathen, Jonothon, Jonothan, Jonothon, Jonathus, Jonty, Zane
Estonian: Ants, Hannus, Johan
French: Jean, Jeanno, Jeannot, Jehan
Gaelic: Eoghan, Eoin, Ian, Seaghan, Seamas, Sean, Shan, Shane, Shawn
German: Anno, Anson, Hanno, Hans, Hanschen, Hansel, Jan, Jens, Johann, Johannes
Greek: Giannakes, Giannes, Giankos, Ioannes, Ioannikos, Jannes, Joannoulos, Joannes, Nannos, Yanni
Hebrew: Jehohanan, Johanan, Yohanan
Hungarian: Ivan, Jani, Janika, Janko, Janos
Irish: Eoghan, Eoin, Owen, Seaghan, Sean, Shan, Shane, Shaun, Shawn
Italian: Gian, Gianni, Giannini, Giannino, Gianozzo, Giovanni, Giovanoli, Nanni, Vanni
Latin: Joannes, Johannes
Lithuanian: Ancas, Enselis, Enskis, Jonas, Jonkus, Jonkuttis
Norwegian: Hans, Jan, Jens, Johan, Jon
Polish: Jan, Janek
Portugese: Joanico, Joaningo, Joao, Joaozinho
Russian: Ivan, Ivanyuschka, Vanechka, Vanka, Vanya, Vanyucha, Vanyushka

139

Scottish: Ian, Iain, Jock, John, Johnnie, Johny
Spanish: Juan, Juanito
Swedish: Jan, Jens, Johan, Jonas, Jonatan
Swiss: Han, Hansli, Johan
Welsh: Evan, Jan, Jenkin, Jevan, Jon, Jones, Sion

A Dictionary of Johns

EVAN (EV'un): **Welsh** form of John. Also, possibly of Celtic origins meaning "young warrior." Ev, Even, Evin, Ewan, Ewen, Owen.

GIOVANNI (Jo VAH'nee): **Italian** form of John. Short forms: Gian, Gianni.

HANS (HAHNS): **German, Dutch,** etc. short form of John, from Johannes.

IAN (EE'an, EE'ahn, or EYE'an): **Scottish** form of John.

IVAN (ee VAHN', EYE'van): **Russian** form of John.

JACK (JAK): Pet form or **nickname** of John. Jackie, Jackson, Jacky.

JAN (YAN) (also pronounced JAN): **Czech, Polish, Dutch,** etc. form of John.

JEAN (ZHAHN) (the final n is nasalized): **French** form of John. Developed in England into the female names, Jane and Jean.

JOCK (JOK): **Scottish nickname** for John, used as familiar name. Jocko, Jocky

JOHANNES (Yo HAHN'nes): **German** form of John, also **Latin** form. Johann and Hans are shortened forms.

JOHN (JON): from the **Hebrew,** Johanan, "God is gracious." Nicknames include Jack, Johnnie, Johnny, Jon.

JON (JON): **Nickname** for John and Jonathan.

JONAS (JOH'nas): **Latin** form of Hebrew name, Jonah, which means "dove." Also **Lithuanian** form of John.

JONATHAN (JON'a thun): **Hebrew** for "God-gave," or "Gift of God." Often associated with John, as in same nickname, Jon.

JUAN (HWAHN, WAHN): **Spanish** form of John.

OWEN (OH'en): **Irish** form of John. Also possibly from **Welsh** name (like Evan) meaning "youth" or "young warrior," and possibly connected with **Latin** and **Greek** forms of Eugene.

SEAN (SHAWN): **Irish** form of John. Also spelled Shawn, Shaun, Shaughn, Shane.

ZANE (ZANE): Usually considered one of the many **English** forms of John. Also possibly connected with **Hebrew** word meaning "ambush," and possibly entering as a first name from a last name.

CHAPTER 18

SPEAKING OF JOHN

John has been such a common name for so long that it has worked its way into the very words we use to describe our world. John, along with the nicknames Jack, Johnny, Jock, and Jockey, has become a part of our language in the form of expressions and descriptions — of people, places, animals, and objects. No other name can claim such a profound influence.

From the slang meanings of "a john" to describe a bathroom and a prostitute's client to such combinations as **longjohns** (long underwear), **jocks** and **jockstraps, lumberjack, jackknife,** and **disc jockeys,** the use of the name John and its variations over the years has been enormous. We've chosen just a few examples here, but we're sure you can think of dozens — even hundreds — more.

JOHN Words:

Dear John Letter

A **Dear John Letter** is a letter written to break off a relationship. The expression arose during World War II as a letter from a soldier's wife asking for a divorce, or from his girlfriend to break off their engagement.

Jack-in-the-Box

A **jack-in-the-box** is a toy in which something (often a clown) springs out of a box unexpectedly. The toy was in use before the early 1700s.

Jackknife

A **jackknife** is a knife whose blade can swing back into the handle. This is also the expression used when the trailer of a truck swings back toward the cab, as well as for a type of dive in swimming.

Jack-o'-lantern

Nothing brings to mind the image of Halloween more than the carved-out pumpkin face of a **jack-o'-lantern.** Over the years the name Jack-o'-lantern, along with other names like will-o-the-wisps, friar's lantern, ignis fatuus (Latin for "foolish fire"), and St. Elmo's Fire, described the phosphorescent lights sometimes seen over swamps and graveyards. Before people knew the lights were actually the spontaneous combustion of gases released by rotting materials, the bluish lights were thought to be magical and mystical. The fires were believed to be wandering spirits who were not allowed into Heaven or Hell and had to carry their own Hell coal fires.

Jackpot

Everyone dreams of winning the **jackpot** — the grand prize, or winning pool. This expression now refers to any situation in which one receives a giant prize or an unexpected reward or achieves the highest level of success. It started out as a poker term, where players can open the pot after they have a pair of jacks or better.

143

Longjohns

Longjohns is the term colloquially used for long underwear. It was the style of boxing clothes worn by the great American boxer, John L. Sullivan.

JOHN Phrases

One of the most popular uses of John phrases is as a description of a type of person. In many countries of the world the typical representative of that country is often referred to by a name; this name is sometimes the name of the country personified. In America we have Uncle Sam (from the letters U.S.), but in Britain **John Bull** is the name for any British man (from John Arbuthnot's satire, *Law is a Bottomless Pit* — 1712. **Ivan Ivanovich** is the typical Russian citizen, and **Johnny Crapaud** (Crapo, Crappo, Crappeau — meaning John Toad) is the typical Frenchman. During the Revolutionary War a patriotic American was known as a **Brother Jonathan.** In addition, **John Q. Public, John Q., John Citizen,** and **John Q. Citizen,** all stand for the typical or average person.

John Doe

Today we call a person whose name is not known **John Doe.** This fictitious name has been used since the fourteenth century. Two witnesses were needed to be present during every legal action. If two witnesses couldn't be found or if the names of the witnesses needed to be protected or kept secret, the names John Doe and Richard Roe were used. Later, in court suits John Doe became the name used instead of the real name of the plaintiff, and Richard Roe was used for the defendant's name. **John-a-Nokes** was another name used like John Doe, and **John-a-Stiles** the Richard Roe substitute.

144

Other appellations have included:

Jack-at-a-pinch

A **Jack-at-a-pinch** is a person who is always there to help out in a time of need.

Jack-of-all-trades

A **Jack-of-all-trades** is one who is good at everything he tries.

Jack-of-both-sides

A **Jack-of-both-sides** (or Jack on both sides) is one who takes both sides of an issue.

Jackass

A **jackass** is a stupid fool.

Johnny-come-lately

A **Johnny-come-lately** (originally Johnny Newcombe, or Johnny Newcome) is a newcomer, or one who is late. Johnny Newcombe was originally the name for a new recruit in the British Navy in the early 1800s; then it came into the American language as Johnny come lately.

Johnny-in-the-middle

A **Johnny-in-the-middle** is someone who acts as mediator between two contending sides.

Johnny-on-the-spot

A **Johnny-on-the-spot** is someone who is always there when needed.

Maxims and Bywords

Variations of "John" appear in many proverbial expressions that have become part of our way of thinking of the world. Some have remained in the language for many years. Others enjoy a much more short-lived popularity. Here are some John maxims and bywords that have shown good staying power:

All work and no play makes Jack a dull boy

One should find a happy medium in life between work and recreation.

Jack of all trades and master of none

If one engages in many different trades, one never becomes skilled at any of them.

Johnny go home!

This is an expression used by natives whenever people flood to a place in search of jobs or fun.

Keeping up with the Joneses

This expression means trying not to be outdone by the neighbors. It was the title of a popular comic strip from 1913-1941, created by Arthur R. Momand.

146

Quick as you can say Jack Robinson!

This expression means in a very short time. It originated in the 1700s after a man named Jack Robinson, who would come to visit his friends and be gone — it was said — before his name was even announced. (The expression predated baseball's Jackie Robinson, known for his fleetness on the basepaths, by about two centuries.)

Animals

Jack, a common nickname of John, has two connotations that often appear in the names of animals: the association of jack with the male of its species and the fact that jack often denotes smallness in size. Young male birds used in falconry were called **jacks.** The young of some kinds of fish, such as pike, are also called **jacks.** Many animals have jack in their name, like **jackrabbit** and **jackass.**

Plants

Some of the more common Johns in the plant world include:

Jack-in-the-pulpit

An American spring herb with a green and purple sheath surrounding an upright floral spike; also the name for many other types of wildflowers. It is also called Indian turnip and was used by North American Indians as a way to determine the fate of a sick patient: If the seed, when placed in a cup of water, floated four times around the cup before sinking, the patient would live. If it sank first, the patient would die. Early settlers used the root in small doses to treat asthma, rheumatism, bronchitis, and ringworm.

147

Johnny-jump-ups

Eurasian pansies *(Viola tricolor)* that have escaped from cultivation and grown wild are called **Johnny-jump-ups.** Usually they have smaller flowers than the cultivated varieties, and they are arranged in different patterns.

Food & Drink

Cracker Jack

Cracker Jack, the candy-coated popcorn and peanut treat, was created in the late 1800s. A German immigrant popcorn stand owner thought that popcorn might make a tasty combination with molasses taffy and peanuts. When one of his friends tasted it, he yelled "That's crackerjack!" (At the time *cracker* was slang for "excellent" or "great" and *Jack* the name for a person whose name is not known; thus "Cracker," "Jack," and "crackerjack" were expressions of approval.)

Johnnycake

Johnnycakes are cakes made from cornmeal, originally on a hot stone, now baked or fried. This popular southern food was quite common in New England in the mid-1800s. There are two possible explanations of the origin of the name. The first is that it was originally called *journey cake* because it was easy to make while one was on a trip. The other is that it was *Shawnee cake,* which the early settlers learned to make from the Shawnee Indians. Eventually it became the similar-sounding johnnycake.

Other foods and drinks include: **jack cheese** (like Monterey jack), a semi-soft cheese, and the brand names for a whiskey, **Jack Daniels,** and a scotch, **Johnny Walker.**

Games

Many games have used John words. The most common association with games is the **Jack** in a deck of cards. In each suit the Jack is the knave (servant) or soldier to the King and Queen. In the card game Euchre the Jack is the highest card.

Black Jack is a popular card game giving the highest honor to the Jack. The small white ball used in lawn bowling as a target is called a **jack. Jacks** is also the name of a popular children's game played with six-pointed "jacks" and a small ball, in which the ball is tossed and the jacks are gathered up.

CHAPTER 19

JOHN IN FICTION

Fiction is often a reflection of the real world and its concerns. So it's not surprising that Johns are just as abundant in the realm of make-believe as they are in the world around us. In stories, songs, books, plays, and the electronic media, we encounter Johns from earliest childhood all through our lives.

For hundreds of years, nursery rhymes and fairy tales have been among the first things a child learns. Of course some of the most popular ones over the years have been about Johns:

Jack and Jill

Jack and Jill went up the hill
To fetch a pail of water;
Jack fell down and broke his crown,
And Jill came tumbling after.

This famous nursery rhyme details the story of a boy and a girl who have come to represent all "lads" and "lasses" in general. Oddly, in a 1765 British woodcut illustrating this rhyme, two boys named **Jack** and Gill are represented; there is no mention of a girl named Jill. The rhyme is believed to have originated in the first half of the seventeenth century. (Only at that time would "water" have rhymed with "after.") Some unconvincing reports have linked the tale to a Norse myth in which two twin children, Hyuki and Bil, accompany Mani, the driver of the chariot of the moon. According to mythology, this lunar pair is supposed to account for the dark spots on the moon.

Jack Be Nimble

Jack be nimble,
Jack be quick,
Jack jumped over
The candlestick.

This popular verse is based on an old British game and method of fortune telling — candlestick jumping. In this traditional custom dating back to the seventeenth century, players jumped over a lighted candle placed on the floor. A person who could jump over it without extinguishing the flame was assured good luck for the coming year. This custom is most closely associated with the festivities that took place on November 25, St. Catherine's Day.

Jack Horner

Little Jack Horner
Sat in the corner,
Eating a Christmas pie;
He put in his thumb,
And pulled out a plum,
And said, "What a good boy am I!"

A legend that has gained popularity over the years suggests that the **Jack Horner** in this rhyme was really Thomas Horner, steward to Richard Whiting, last of the abbots of Glastonbury. At the time, Henry VIII had claimed much of the Church property as his own. Whiting sent his steward to the king with a Christmas gift, intended to appease His Highness: a pie containing the concealed deeds to twelve manorial estates. Although Horner's descendants deny it, legend claims that on the way to London, the steward pulled out the deed to the manor of Mells, where his descendants reside even to this day.

Jack Sprat

Jack Sprat could eat no fat,
His wife could eat no lean,
And so between them both, you see,
They licked the platter clean.

Originally titled **"Jack Prat,"** a sixteenth- and seventeenth-century name for a dwarf, this rhyme has a history of revisions. It seems to have been a familiar proverbial rhyme, appearing twice in **John Clarke**'s proverb collection in 1639 and in James Howell's collection twenty years later. Finally, in 1670, the verse was recorded in its present form by **John Ray.** Since then, several other modified versions have been produced, but the one offered here is the most familiar.

Hansel and Gretel

Hansel and Gretel is an old German fairy tale recorded by the nineteenth-century folklorists, Jakob and Wilhelm Grimm. The story is about the two children of a woodcutter whose family has nothing but a loaf of bread to eat. Realizing that there is not enough to go around, the children's stepmother convinces her husband to leave **Hansel** and his sister Gretel deep in the forest. While wandering in the woods, the two hungry travelers happen upon the gingerbread house of an old witch. The witch invites them to stay for dinner, but she has something else in mind. She locks Hansel in the stable, and prepares to cook the children for her next meal. While she opens the oven, Gretel pushes the witch inside, and rescues her brother. The children take the witch's jewels and find their way back home.

Jack and the Beanstalk

Jack and the Beanstalk is a traditional folk tale that is found in varying forms among many cultures all around the world. According to the English version, **Jack** trades his poor mother's cow in exchange for a handful of beans, one of which miraculously sprouts into a plant that extends into the heavens. Climbing to the top of the beanstalk, Jack discovers a giant's castle, from which he steals bags of money, a harp, and a red hen that lays golden eggs. In order to escape the angry giant, who has followed him down the beanstalk, Jack chops down the great plant, sending the giant to his death. This symbolic tale is derived from a Norse myth, in which man (Jack) receives gifts from a giant (All-father) at the top of the great beanstalk (Yggdrasil), bringing him great wealth (verdure).

Jack Frost

Jack Frost, the personification of icy weather, is pictured in children's stories and songs as an elflike character who traces the beautiful frost patterns on trees and windowpanes. In Norse myths, he was *Jokul* ("icicle"), also called *Frosti* ("frost"), the son of Kari, the god of the winds. Russian myths picture the frost spirit as a white-haired old smith, *Father Frost,* who binds the earth and water with his icy chains. German folktales describe *Old Mother Frost,* who shakes out a cloud of white feathers when she makes her bed, causing the snow to fall.

As we grew older and read novels and other adult books, we found still more Johns:

Ivan Denisovich

Russian writer Alexander Solzhenitsyn's novel, *One Day in the Life of Ivan Denisovich,* portrays a young man, convicted of treason, who relates the horrors of imprisonment in a Russian concentration camp. The situation is described through the eyes of **Ivan Denisovich** who takes the reader through the day as he explains how he tries to fight the cold of twenty below while wearing only rags. He must also find ways to scrounge up enough food to eat, among other problems. With the rising of the moon at the end of the novel, it becomes apparent that Ivan Denisovich has once again survived another day.

Don Juan

Don Juan, fiction's greatest legendary lover, is the hero of several works of literature by classical writers like Molière and Lord Byron. In these works, Don Juan travels from one place to the next, seducing women wherever he goes. His witty sense of humor and arrogant courage make him a universal scandalous philanderer. In most versions, this reckless conduct brings about both his fame and his downfall. Curiously, Don Juan is also the name of the Toltee Indian teacher in Carlos Castenada's philosophical, sociological novels, which include *A Separate Reality, The Teachings of Don Juan,* and *The Eagle's Gift.*

Little John

In the folk tale, *Robin Hood,* **Little John** is first introduced as a tall stranger that Robin Hood encounters at a bridge. The two scuffle and later compete in a shooting match, which Robin wins. The stranger, dubbed Little John because he is so big, acknowledges defeat and becomes a member of Robin's band. In the course of the tale, Little John is involved in numerous adventures with Robin Hood's band, stealing from the rich and giving to the poor. When Robin Hood finally meets his end, only Little John is there with him. As a last request, Robin asks to be buried wherever his last arrow lands. Little John faithfully marks the arrow's path and carries out his promise.

Long John Silver

Robert Louis Stevenson's *Treasure Island* is one of the great classics for children. In this novel **Long John Silver** is immortalized as one of the most famous pirates in literature. Originally hired as the ship's cook for *The Hispaniola,* Silver organizes a mutiny, and transforms the crew into a pirate band in search of treasure on a deserted island. He is portrayed as a smooth-talking, authoritative figure with only one leg. Although he does not share in the treasure in the end, he does escape to the West Indies with a bag of coins.

Jean Valjean

The popular Broadway musical *Les Misérables* is based on Victor Hugo's novel of the same name. It is the story of a criminal, **Jean Valjean,** who is used by the author to point out the misery and contradictions of the society in which he lived. Imprisoned for stealing a loaf of bread for his starving sister, Valjean was sentenced to hard labor in the galleys; an escape attempt increased his term to nineteen years. Freed at last, he found all doors closed to an "ex-convict." Taking an assumed name, he became popular and successful as Father Madeleine. When his true identity was revealed, he lost everything and became a hunted man. It is interesting to note that his name is a contraction of "Jean Voilà Jean," meaning "John, there's John."

Dr. John Watson

"Elementary, my dear Watson," the world's most famous detective assures his faithful sidekick. In Arthur Conan Doyle's popular Sherlock Holmes novels, the excitable Dr. **John Watson** is the human foil for the idealized intellectual, Sherlock Holmes. All of the emotions bottled up inside the calm, cool-headed Holmes are expressed through Dr. Watson. Throughout the stories, Watson stumbles over baffling clues and presents them to his companion, who remains undaunted as he attempts to piece them together.

155

In *The Sign of Four,* Dr. Watson falls in love with the pretty client, Miss Mary Morstran. Once the mystery is solved, Watson declares his love for her and proposes marriage. She accepts his proposal, and the two receive the good wishes of Sherlock Holmes.

Television and the movies have had their fair share of characters named John:

J.R. Ewing

Dallas is one of the most popular prime-time serials ever to appear on TV. But it would never have achieved such smashing success without its villainous millionaire, **John Ross Ewing,** J.R. — "The man America loves to hate." Played by Larry Hagman, J.R. shocked his audiences as he struggled for wealth and power, destroying his family and friends in the process. In the series' most successful ploy, J.R. was shot in the chest at the end of the 1979-1980 season. The resulting "Who shot J.R.?" mystery made headlines all over the world. In order to preserve the identity of the attempted murderer, five alternative conclusions were filmed with five different cast members pulling the trigger. On November 21, 1980, it was finally revealed in the single most widely watched TV program up to that time that Kristen, his wife's younger sister, was the attempted murderer. As it turned out, J.R. was only wounded, not killed — T.V.'s most cherished villain lives on!

Dear John

The surprise hit of the 1988-1989 season was a situation comedy called *Dear John,* about a support group of lonely singles who meet each week in a community center. *Dear John* is centered around the life of **John Lacey** (played by Judd Hirsch of *Taxi),* a divorced man whose wife left him a Dear John letter saying she'd run off with his ex-best friend. The shows are written by John Sullivan, who created the characters for a BBC series with the same name.

Trapper John, M.D.

This TV series, starring Pernell Roberts as Dr. **John (Trapper) McIntyre,** began in the fall season of 1979. Trapper John, who works at the San Francisco Memorial Hospital, was originally featured in *M*A*S*H*, one of TV's most popular sitcoms, where he was played by Wayne Rogers. This previous existence is occasionally alluded to in the newer series.

John Steed

Though first broadcast in England in 1961, the comic British spy series, *The Avengers,* was not shown in America until 1966. It starred Patrick Macnee as **John Steed,** a well-mannered intellectual working as a government agent. Steed, with amateur partner Emma Peel, an adventurous woman whose leather attire was in striking contrast to Steed's three-piece suit and bowler, appeared in fifty-one episodes before the series was taken off the air in September 1969. Steed later reappeared in the fall of 1978 on *The New Avengers,* this time without his female sidekick.

John-Boy Walton

In late December 1971, CBS broadcasted a Christmas special entitled "The Homecoming" featuring Earl Hamner Jr.'s Waltons, a close-knit family living in Virginia during the Depression. The special was so well received that CBS created a series around the family called *The Waltons.* In the series, different actors were chosen for three of the four Walton adults, but all of the seven children remained the same. One of the children was John Walton Jr., the eldest son, played by Richard Thomas. Nicknamed **John-Boy,** this character became a talented writer like his creator, and it is through his narration that we learn about how life was on Walton Mountain.

John Rambo

When the movie *First Blood* appeared, its hero, **John Rambo,** tapped into a vein of deep feeling and became an instant cliché. But as novelist David Morrell, Rambo's original creator, points out, those who characterize Rambo as a macho symbol of military violence gone out of control have misunderstood him. Rambo, as visualized and portrayed by actor Sylvester Stallone, is a man of complex emotions, pushed to the edge and forced to respond with violence; yet his reactions are reluctant and tempered, and he uses violence only as a last resort. Rambo, incidentally, did not have a first name in the 1972 novel in which he originated. "John" was added in the movie, drawing on the allusions to *When Johnny Comes Marching Home.*

Tarzan, the Ape Man

When *Tarzan of the Apes* first came out as a novella in *All Story* magazine in 1912, Edgar Rice Borroughs never expected the story to sell. But **John Clayton,** Lord Greystoke, better known as Tarzan, became the most successful hero in American fiction. In the story, Clayton became the adopted son of Kala, a female ape who called him Tarzan, meaning "white skin." The famous cry of Tarzan used in the popular Tarzan movies featuring Olympic swimmer Johnny Weissmuller was created by combining five separate sound tracks into one recording: a dog's growl, a soprano note sung by Lorraine Bridges, a note from the G-string of a violin, a hyena cry run backwards, and Weissmuller's own rendering of the war cry.

Musical Johns

Even songs have their Johns, from the stirring Civil War song, "When **Johnny** Comes Marching Home," to the ballads of memorable heroes like **John Henry** and **Casey Jones** (whose real name was John Luther Jones) and the abolitionist **John Brown,**

158

whose "body lies a-mouldering in his grave." Modern songs about Johns include Chuck Berry's classic rock'n'roll hit **"Johnny B. Goode,"** the Shelley Fabares hit **"Johnny** Angel," and the Beach Boys' "Sloop **John B."**

The Ballad of John Henry

The introduction of machines to replace manpower generated great resentment among railroad workers in the late nineteenth century. In an attempt to prove man's superiority over machines, a strong black, **John Henry,** pitted himself against the steam-driven piston drill that was threatening to replace him. In a contest that lasted thirty-five minutes, John Henry proved to be the victor, driving his drill through fourteen feet of hard rock while the machine cut through only nine. Soon after, however, he died of a heart attack, "with a hammer in his hand." Several versions of "The Ballad of John Henry" were written in his honor.

Johnny B. Goode

One of the most influential performers in Rock and Roll history, Chuck Berry, rocked the stage with unflagging enthusiasm. His hit single, **"Johnny B. Goode"** in 1958, was about a guitar player very much like Berry himself. In Chuck Berry's words, Johnny B. Goode played the guitar "like he was ringin' a bell," causing everyone to call after him, "Go! Go Johnny, go!" This song, along with his numerous other hits, helped to create the Rock and Roll that has become so popular today.

When Johnny Comes Marching Home

"When Johnny Comes Marching Home" was originally published as "Johnny Fill Up the Bowl" in 1863. This popular Civil War song is generally credited to Union Army bandmaster Patrick Sarsfield Gilmore under the pseudonym Louis Lambert. Some historians, however, believe that it came from an old Irish jig. Whatever the case, Gilmore's version became one of the strong-est and most widely known songs of that period. In its original form, it was quite unusual: It is one of only a few songs in a minor key to attain such wide acceptance and popularity. A Broadway musical based on the song opened in the winter of 1902.

CHAPTER 20

NONHUMAN JOHNS

A Commemorative Name

John is more than just a name for people. All around us, countless things we see every day — foods, objects, groups, buildings, stores, airports, streets, cities, mountains, rivers, and islands — have been named in commemoration of Johns who touched or changed the world in some way.

Cereals, Sandwiches and Cigarettes . . .

Kellogg's Corn Flakes is an all-American breakfast tradition which has been around since **Dr. John Kellogg** introduced it in 1907. Getty oil stations seen all across the country are a constant reminder of the great oil magnate **J. Paul Getty,** who became one of the richest men ever. The sandwich was named after **John Montagu,** fourth earl of Sandwich, and the geiger counter after German physicist **Hans Geiger.** McIntosh apples were named after Canadian **John McIntosh,** and nicotine after a Frenchman, **Jean Nicot.**

Schools, Churches and Airports . . .

All around the country, institutions, schools, and other notable places like Cape Kennedy, JFK International Airport, and the Kennedy Space Center were named as a tribute to **John F. Kennedy,** America's 35th President. The notable business tycoon and philanthropist, **John D. Rockefeller,** is another well known John with countless commemorations — the most famous, perhaps, being Rockefeller Center in New York City. Churches throughout the world were dedicated to the Saints **John the Apostle** and **John the Baptist.**

John Universities

There are many dozens of schools and universities named for Johns. The most famous are Harvard University, founded in 1636 and named after the school's first benefactor, **John Harvard,** and Johns Hopkins University, named after a Quaker banker named **Johns Hopkins.**

Groups Named John

Many groups and organizations also have John in their name. **The John Birch Society** and the many **Jockey Clubs** found throughout the world are two of the most well known.

Places Named John

The list of places named John around the world is almost endless. In the United States, nearly half the states contain a Johnson County. One of the most famous John cities is Johannesburg in South Africa, which was named after two Johns, **Johann Rissik** and **Johannes Joubert,** in 1896. The mere mention of the city's name conjures up a whole assortment of images — from gold and safaris to apartheid and bitter conflict.

Three Floods Too Many

In the U.S., Johnstown has been in the news more times than its inhabitants would like. The unhappy claim to fame for this city in Pennsylvania is based on three floods that struck in 1889, 1936, and 1977, claiming many lives. The town was named in 1834 after its founder, **Joseph Johns.**

Kool-Aid Massacre

The mention of another place — Jonestown — brings back even worse memories. Named after cult leader **Jim Jones,** this place in Guyana became world famous after the much publicized "Kool-Aid Massacre," which claimed over 900 lives and set the world investigating countless other cult groups.

Home of the Swallows

On a more cheerful note, San Juan Capistrano, a historic mission in California named after the crusader **St. John of Capistrano,** is known for its swallows, which arrive in great chirping flocks on St. Joseph's Day (March 19) and leave promptly on St. John's Day (October 23), amidst tourist festivals and celebrations.

Horses Named John

In the world of animals, Johns certainly rank among the most interesting. **Clever Hans** was the famous horse who had nineteenth-century scientists and psychologists baffled by his ability to perform mathematical computations by tapping out the answers with his hooves. Another famous horse was **Black Jack,** the lone, riderless horse that followed John F. Kennedy's coffin during his funeral.

Baboons and Lions . . .

Jack the Baboon became famous in the late 1800s by helping his crippled master as a railroad signalman. For nine years Jack worked for a salary of twenty cents and a day and half a bottle

163

of beer on Saturdays. Another baboon, **Jackie,** was not only a mascot in World War I but also an important scout that warned his human comrades when the enemy was approaching. After the war he received an honorable discharge from his South African regiment, with papers describing him as "bilingual." **Jackie** was also the name of a popular lion actor who played MGM's trademark for eighteen years.

Are Chimps as Smart as Humans?

One of the earliest chimpanzee intelligence tests involved a chimp named **Joni** in Russia. Nadia Kohts compared Joni's development up to the age of four with that of her own son, and discovered that although there are many similarities, humans are more intelligent than chimps.

Fictional Animal Johns

The world of fiction has its share of animals named John. **Jack Rabbit** and **Jack Hare** are two of the most common names found in fables and folk tales. A more recent famous fictional bunny was the **Jack Hare** in Kit Williams' book, *Masquerade* —the story of a rabbit who sets out to find a treasure. In the book were clues that led a lucky person to find a real-life treasure!

Jonathan Livingston Seagull is perhaps the most famous fictional animal of modern times. This allegorical tale is the story of a seagull searching for the meaning of life.

CHAPTER 21

JOHN TRIVIA

John Who?

Match these famous Johns to their nicknames:

1. John Quincy Adams

2. Johann Sebastian Bach

3. Johnny Carson

4. John Ehrlichman

5. John Gilbert

6. John Paul I

7. J. P. Morgan

8. John L. Sullivan

9. John Tyler

10. John O'Hara

A. The Great Squeaky Lover

B. The Boston Strong Boy

C. The Voice of The Hangover Generation

D. Second John

E. The Prince of Darkness

F. The Great Khan of Wall Street

G. The Hanging Judge

H. The Smiling Pope

I. The Old Wig

J. The Whitehouse Fireman

Match These Sobriquets
to the Johns Who Earned Them

1. Father & Glory of Boston

2. Father of Chicago

3. Father of Greater Philadelphia

4. Father of Massachusetts

5. Father of New England

6. Father of London

7. Father of Rhode Island

8. Father of American Botany

9. Father of American Independence

10. Father of the American Navy

11. Father of the American Baptists

12. Father of English Prose

13. Father of English Unitarianism

14. Father of French Philosophy

15. Father of Swedish Music

16. Father of Printing

17. Father of Sentiment

18. Father of New Economics

A. Johann Gutenberg

B. John Clarke

C. John Endicott

D. John Barry

E. Jean-Jacques Rousseau

F. John Winthrop

G. Johan Roman

H. John Clarke

I. John Maynard Keynes

J. John Cotton

K. John Wycliffe

L. John Bartram

M. John Barnard

N. Jean Baptiste Point Du Sable

O. John Biddle

P. John Christian Bullitt

Q. Jean le Rond D'Alembert

R. John Adams

Who Said That?

Match these famous quotes to the Johns who said them:

1. "Baby you're the greatest."

2. "No man is an island."

3. "We're more popular than Jesus Christ now."

4. "We stand today on the edge of a new frontier."

5. "So many beautiful women and so little time."

6. "I can't afford to waste my time making money."

7. "Anybody has the right to evade taxes if he can get away with it."

8. "Collecting more taxes than is absolutely necessary is legalized robbery."

9. "The future of Labor is the future of America."

10. "Blessed be he who expects nothing, for he shall never be disappointed.

A. John F. Kennedy

B. John L. Lewis

C. J(ohn) P. Morgan

D. Jackie Gleason

E. Jonathan Swift

F. (John) Calvin Coolidge

G. John Donne

H. John Barrymore

I. (Jean) Louis Agassiz

J. John Lennon

Alias John Doe

These Johns are better known by what name?

1. Carmen Orrico
2. Walter Palanuik
3. Julius Garfinkle
4. John F. Sullivan
5. Sean O'Feeney

A. Fred Allen
B. John Ford
C. Jack Palance
D. John Saxon
E. John Garfield

Hidden Johns

```
J   O   H   N   J   O   N   E   S   J

E   E   W   A   U   B   W   C   O   O

V   D   A   E   A   E   E   H   F   N

A   Z   W   N   N   G   N   H   S   A

N   A   N   N   O   S   I   N   H   T

N   N   J   K   J   L   M   A   A   H

S   E   A   N   N   I   A   I   N   A

I   N   N   A   V   O   I   G   E   N

J   O   N   I   J   A   C   K   I   E

Y   O   H   A   N   A   N   J   A   N
```

Can you find these variations of the name John in the puzzle above?

Evan	Jan	Juan
Ewan	Jean	Nannos
Ewen	John	Owen
Gian	Johns	Sean
Giovanni	Jon	Shane
Iain	Jonathan	Yohanan
Ian	Jones	Zane
Jackie	Joni	

Match These Famous Johns
to Their Former Occupations

1. Pope John Paul II (Catholic Pope)

2. John Chancellor (news reporter)

3. Sean Connery (actor)

4. Jonathan Winters (comedian)

5. John Huston (director)

A. bricklayer

B. boxer

C. fruit picker

D. carpenter's assistant

E. factory worker

Scrambled John

These words and sentences are really people's names all jumbled up. Can you rearrange the letters to come up with a famous person named John? (Hint: Remove all punctuation.)

1. NAIL A JAR MUCH?

2. NO ADJOURNING POEM.

3. OH BLOW THIN JOKES!

4. JOLT ON HAND

5. LET HIM JOIN SERVILE ARTS.

6. AND NOW A MAN GOES THROUGH A GOLF MAZE.

7. HE'S NOW JILL.

8. IF MEN ALIGN...

9. OH, NJ STEAK!

10. NEVER JAR ME!

Crypto-Johns

These jumbled-up letters really spell out a quote by a famous person named John. In each quote, every letter of the alphabet has been replaced by a different letter, and the substitution is consistent for the entire quote. Figure out the "code" for the real letters, and you will unravel the hidden quotation.

1. "HIOTBHKN HQRPOTKOK HQ IHPORA JPYJPAHYQ AY YQOK IHKATQRO DPYN AZO JPYEBON." — MYZQ STBKUYPAZC, OQSBHKZ UPHAOP

2. "BCSDS EDS YVBR VW HSVHYS PCV MEK'B BCQKF RSDQVGRYX PQBCVGB QKZGDQKJ BCSQD TQKAR." — ZVCK ZEX MCEHTEK, ETSDQMEK PDQBSD

3. "CSN ASF'D YUWJ DS KNXXJE DS GR U BSJD. UASVJKPJFPJ TK KNXXJETFR JFSNRY XSE UFZSFJ." — CSYF PTUEAT, UHJETPUF BSJD

4. "J EOPOZXRFO RD J TOXDVI GLV GVXND LJXM JPP LRD PRNO FV ZOEVBO GOPP NIVGI, FLOI GOJXD MJXN APJDDOD FV JUVRM ZORIA XO EVAIRQOM." — WXOM JPPOI (CVLI W. DKPPRUJI), JBOXREJI EVBOMRJI

5. "DAVJV EU AMJLGT MKTDAEKI EK DAV HYJGL DAMD UYNV NMK ZMKKYD NMRV M GEDDGV HYJUV, MKL UVGG M GEDDGV ZAVMBVJ." — SYAK JOUREK, XJEDEUA HJEDVJ MKL MJD ZJEDEZ

170

Name That John

1.

2.

3.

4.

5.

Crossword Puzzles

Puzzle 1

Across

1. Gretel's German brother
6. The bird painter
9. One of England's greatest landscape painters
15. John Law's downfall: _____ money or " _____ Chase"
16. Wolfman Jack's musical occupation
18. John Travolta in "Saturday Night _____"

19. Magazine edited by John W. Campbell
20. British ship that fired on John Paul Jones
21. Jackie Gleason — "The Great _____ "

Down

1. Comic strip cartoonist
2. John Paul Jones' real answer when asked to surrender
3. Wolfman Jack moved from Mexico to a station in _____
4. You won't find Ed McBain on Evan Hunter's _____
5. "Sanford _____ Son"
7. Italian Renaissance painter
8. Colonial portrait artist
10. _____ Grapes of Wrath
11. "Saturday Night _____ " or " _____ and Let Die"
12. "The _____ Falcon, directed by John Huston
14. Jackie Stewart popularized this sport
16. Jackson Pollock liked to _____ paint on his canvases
17. Famous name

Puzzle 2

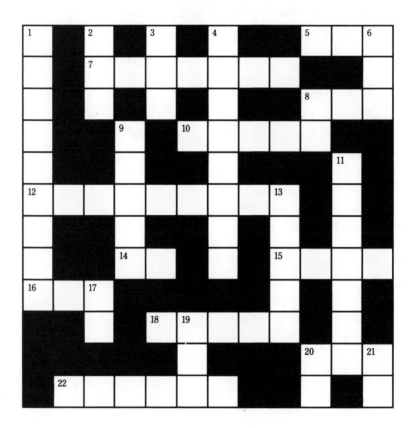

Across

5. 007 creator's initials
7. Heavy Metal's nice guy
8. Jean-Claude Killy certainly knows how to _____
10. He controlled the first U.S. monopoly
12. Ernst was the middle name of this American writer
14. You can see John Forsythe on _____
15. Ans and Janke are the _____ forms of John
16. If you're going to have a lover, Jean-Baptiste Poquelin suggests you get along with this animal
18. The "stingy" comedian with a big heart: Jack _____

20. John Barrymore said "Sex is not taxed — _____ it can be taxing."
22. Some consider him the greatest quarterback ever

Down

1. Jonathan Chapman's better known surname
2. John Akers keeps this corporate giant ahead of the competition
3. Hall _____ Oates
4. He is most famous for his autobiography, Confessions
6. J. Edgar Hoover's home away from home
8. John D. Rockefeller, Jr.'s father
9. Ireland's greatest satirist — Jonathan _____
11. We have this John to thank for sandwiches
13. This skier won the triple crown in the 1987 Olympics
17. John Welsh Jr. is the Chairman of this electrifying company
19. Juan Peron's wife Evita's real name
20. "Blessed _____ he who expects nothing, for he shall never _____ disappointed"
21. "You" (French; form Madame de Warens would have used to Rousseau)

More John Trivia!

Scrambled Johns

These words and sentences are really people's names all jumbled up. Can you rearrange the letters to come up with a famous person named John? (Hint: Remove all punctuation.)

1. DANNVILLE

2. I CAN JOKE, ROB, SIN!

3. I STACK JET WARE.

4. JOIN ANY HUNTS?

5. JOAN HAS MD.

6. BITTER NAVEL HEIR

7. SHE WILL, JON.

8. HEY, JON WED.

9. UGLY PAN EAT JET.

10. HE HAS NO BLIN.

11. HE IN LUSH JOB.

12. DRY HEN ON DJ.

13. AN EVEN HURT.

14. NO-JOCK LAND.

15. ARGH, NO FOG ON LAND, MAW, JUST A MAZE. AMAZED G-MAN WON TON JAR OF LAUGHS.

16. REAL JAPAN PREMIER.

17. SEE TEAM IN PERIL AT JOB.

18. ANGRY "ZEE"

19. CON EARNS YEN.

Who Said That?

Match these famous quotes with the Johns who said them:

1. "Ask not what your country can do for you — ask what you can do for your country."

2. "He who moves not forward goes backward."

3. "Help yourself, and heaven will help you."

4. "Here I am at the end of the road and at the top of the heap."

5. "How sweet it is!"

6. "There's none so blind as they that won't see.

7. "No man who knows aught, can be so stupid to deny that all men naturally were born free."

8. "Everything of importance in this world has been accomplished by the free inquiring spirit."

9. "The best philanthropy is a search for cause, an attempt to cure evils at their source."

A. Jean de la Fontaine

B. Jackie Gleason

C. Johann von Goethe

D. Pope John XXIII

E. John F. Kennedy

F. John L. Lewis

G. John Milton

H. John D. Rockefeller, Sr.

I. Jonathan Swift

Trivia Quiz

1. Which U.S. Vice Presidents were members of the "John Clan."? Include both first names and surnames.

2. What famous John had a son nicknamed John-John?

3. What popular singer uses the name of a historical John?

4. What U.S. President was named after a religious leader?

5. What fictional animal was named after a religious leader?

6. Who shared the 1954 Nobel Prize for pioneering research that laid the foundation for the development of a polio vaccine?

7. What major league baseball player has the same name as the founder of a famous restaurant/hotel chain?

8. How many "double Johns" can you name? (People whose first and last names are both variations of John.)

9. What director, previously known mainly for plumbing the depths of bad taste, had an unexpected hit with his film, *Hairspray*?

10. What furniture style was named after a notable John?

Crypto-Johns

These jumbled-up letters really spell out a quote by a famous person named John. In each quote, every letter of the alphabet has been replaced by a different letter, and the substitution is consistent for the entire quote. Figure out the "code" for real letters, and you will unravel the hidden quotation.

1. "PLUGXI GPALH LUA SGCA ENAHHKAX KVMAP WVUFLUP RNAJ KLJ QA QALRAX QBR RNAJ KLJ HRLUR L FGXXGXI ILKA." — TVNLXX FVSWILXI MVX IVARNA, IAUKLX FUGRAU

2. "BGT YQB BNA PHGYWGYI BNXB GT BQ EA ECXKAP, EMB BNA AJRATT." — ZQNY TACPAY, AYICGTN ZMPIA

3. "FXCT I VIT GB FOIDDCV RD GT XGVBCAN, XC VILCB I DOCMMK BVIAA DIELISC." — ZJXT ORBLGT, CTSAGBX IOM EOGMGE

4. "FAID AZ G NJGODKL IRJ NTRZD QTR IDDF, GEK G CRVDKL IRJ NTRZD QTR NTAEY." — MDGE KD FG SJXLDJD, IJDECT QJANDJ

5. "DA SBJQ IANCALA CH NBPX. UTG FTD ANJA PVH DA AMYNVCH QFA JBPPAJJ TU QFTJA DA ETH'Q NCXA." — ZAVH PTPQAVB, UGAHPF DGCQAG, UCNSSVXAG

179

Crossword Puzzle

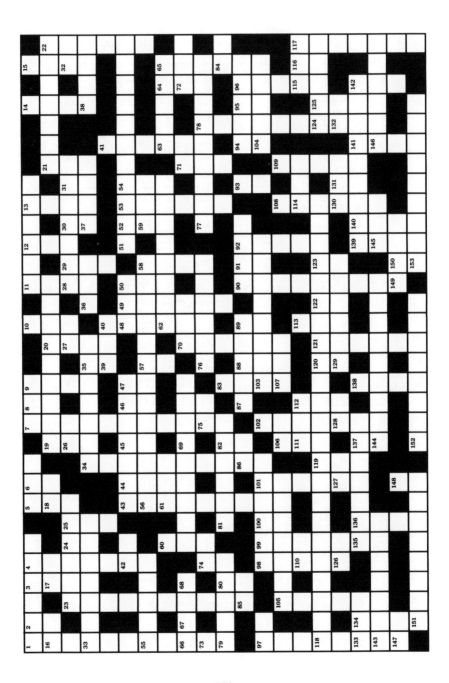

Across

1. *The Disinherited* by Jack ———
5. Bon ———
7. "Leaving on a ——— Plane"
11. "Black ———" by Terence Dudley
16. *The Wonder City of* ——— by Jack Snow
17. ———. White (Initials)
18. Associated Press (abbreviation)
19. John Adams' pen name
21. Jack, formerly Jean-Louis, ———
23. Hardly what you'd call a Cadillac
26. "———? What'd you say?"
27. Middle English second person nominative plural
28. *Appointment in* ——— by John O'Hara
32. New Hampshire (abbreviation)
33. Teaching an old word a new trick
34. Otherwise known as a custodian
36. Dracula's alter ego
37. ——— truly yours
38. "I think that I shall never see a billboard lovely as a ———." — Ogden Nash

Down

1. The ——— Wits (John Trumbull was one)
2. *Lucky Bucky in* ——— by John R. Neill
3. ——— estate
4. Abuse
5. ——— bees don't fly in September
6. Out of print (abbreviation)
7. His book *Fanny Hill* figured in the first known American obscenity case
8. Baum's Land of ———
9. Tense
10. Alcoholic beverage brewed from malt and hops
11. To pile Pelion upon ———
12. A rotating piece which imparts motion to a roller moving against its edge
13. Concerning (phrase)
14. "The Owl and the Pussy-cat went to sea In a beautiful pea-green ———," — Edward Lear
15. Novel by Jean Toomer that started the Harlem Renaissance
19. National Education Association (abbreviation)

Across (cont'd)

39. Used to catch a fish
42. Not them, but ———
43. Shakespeare's Venetian Moor
48. Bishop's ——— *of Darkness*
51. Harry Patterson's Library of Congress listing
55. Flavorful
56. A book by Hans Christian Andersen considered "smut" in Illinois
59. "The dragon's ——— more fierce than fire / Laid low their towers and houses frail." —J. R. R. Tolkien
61. European Economic Community (abbreviation)
62. Never off the bestseller lists, 1917-1925
63. The S in NEWS
66. "——— into the garden, Maud" — Tennyson
68. "——— : A Tale" by Poe
70. Not near

Down (cont'd)

20. "Twas brillig, and the slithy toves / Did ——— and gimble in the wabe." — Lewis Carroll
21. The letter "k"
22. Dairy product
23. Infamous head of the New York Society for the Suppression of Vice
24. Original gum (abbreviation)
25. A small box
29. "And Ceasar's spirit, ranging for revenge, / With ——— at his side, come hot from hell" — Shakespeare
31. Railroad (abbreviation)
34. He wrote *The Glastonbury Romance*
35. ——— *Trial* by Elmer Rice
40. Alias John Clayton
41. What the snake did
43. His story lies behind Melville's *Moby Dick*
44. Exercise: to touch your ———
45. Education (abbreviation)
46. Lower right (abbreviation)

Across (cont'd)

71. "_____ virtuous and you will be eccentric." — Mark Twain
72. Clod
73. Characteristic of the upper class
74. "Let _____ be finale of seem." — Wallace Stevens
75. North Dakota (abbreviation)
76. Jack _____, author and oyster pirate
77. Alias
79. Joyce Kilmer's famous ditty
81. Unfrozen
84. Los Angeles (abbreviation)
85. Egyptian sun god
86. Yukon Territory (abbreviation)
87. To give a speech
90. Decree
94. John _____ Bishop
97. Final copy (abbreviation)
98. John Dos _____ (author)
103. 1923 Pulitzer Prize-winning drama by Owen Davis

Down (cont'd)

47. Left eye (abbreviation)
49. John _____, poet
50. _____ *Nights in a Barroom* by T.S. Arthur
53. Wrinkle
54. A _____ *to Uncle Tom's Cabin* by Harriet Beecher Stowe
57. "_____ Helen" by Poe
58. "I have _____ the future, and it works." —Lincoln Steffens
60. _____ *U.P. Trail* by Zane Grey
64. Child's play
65. This Shakespearean drama was first performed in America at the John Street Theater
67. Exclamation used to express surprise
69. Lethal dose (abbreviation)
70. This John provided the art for the first illustrated book in America
71. "None _____ the brave deserve the fair." —John Dryden
74. Hogwash
78. He wrote *The Virginian*

Down (cont'd)

80. _____. Robinson (initials)
82. _____ Extraterrestrial (abbreviation)
83. The _____ Reaper
88. "He played the King as though under the momentary apprehension that someone else was about to play the _____."
—Eugene Field on Creston Clarke as King Lear
89. Eastbound (abbreviation)
90. John Crowe Ransom was one of these
91. _____ like Flynn
92. *A Bell for* _____ by John Hersey
93. "_____, the people . . ."
94. Psychokinesis (abbreviation)
95. One (dialect form)
96. The camel's no-hump cousin
97. John Gould _____ (poet)
98. A metrical foot with one stressed and three unstressed syllables
99. John James _____ (author, naturalist)
100. South Carolina (abbreviation)

Across (cont'd)

104. Not kneeled but _____
105. *The Life and Times of* _____ by John Gardner
106. "Et _____, Brute?"
107. *La* _____, composed by Achille-Claude Debussy
110. Editor (abbreviation)
111. The rowan, or mountain _____
114. The Harding administration objected to this work by Upton Sinclair
115. A treasure _____
118. John Patrick's 1954 Pulitzer Prize-winning drama
124. To cut violently
126. Latin abbreviation for "Note well."
127. Poetic expression meaning "Behold!"
128. Capote's _____ *Cold Blood*
129. Wordy
130. By way of
132. "_____ Deum"

184

Down (cont'd)

101. The Maryland state bird
102. Easier
105. Gregorian _____
106. Tit for _____
108. *Self-Portrait in a* _____ *Mirror* by John Ashberry
109. John _____, Poe's stepfather
113. The Dynamic _____
116. _____ the world turns
117. John Wheatley's poetic slave
119. _____ *Whom the Bell Tolls* by Hemingway
112. Madder than a wet _____
120. _____ *the Down Staircase* by Bel Kaufman
121. _____ Allen, comedienne
122. Sea level (abbreviation)
123. _____ missile
125. "_____, Kindly Light" by Cardinal Newman
131. That is (abbreviation)

Across (cont'd)

133. "Love in a _____, with water a crust, Is — Love forgive us! — cinders, ashes, dust." — John Keats
135. "You see, but you do not _____." — Sir Arthur Conan Doyle
139. John _____ Whittier (poet)
143. *The Private Life of Helen of Troy* by John
144. Whittier's "Barbara _____"
145. Expression of negation
146. A great trial
147. Rhode Island (abbreviation)
149. Easter or trained _____
151. This John's mother was Margaret Fuller's niece
152. This John collected quotes
153. This John won a prize for his grapes

Down (cont'd)

134. _____ and Thummim
136. Alpha, _____, gamma, delta
137. Very fine (abbreviation)
138. A _____ of strength
139. "Blind guides, which strain at a _____
     and swallow a camel." — Matthew 23:24
141. "There is a book, who runs may read,
     Which heavenly truth imparts
     And all the _____ its scholars need,
     Pure eyes and Christian hearts." —
     John Keble
142. "Once did she hold the gorgeous East in
     _____." — Wordsworth
148. Year of the Lord (abbreviation)
150. Einsteinium (abbreviation)

John Trivia Answers

John Who (p.165)

1. D
2. I
3. E
4. J
5. A
6. H
7. F
8. B
9. G
10. C

Who Said That? (p. 167)

1. D
2. G
3. J
4. A
5. H
6. I
7. C
8. F
9. B
10. E

Alias John Doe (p. 167)

1. D
2. C
3. E
4. A
5. B

Father Sobriquets (p. 166)

1. J
2. N
3. P
4. F
5. C
6. M
7. H
8. L
9. R
10. D
11. B
12. K
13. O
14. Q
15. G
16. A
17. E
18. I

Hidden Johns (p. 168)

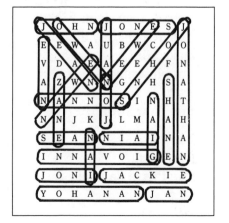

Occupations (p. 169)

1. E   2. D   3. A   4. C   5. B

Scrambled Johns (p. 169)

1. Juan Marichal
2. Juan Domingo Peron
3. John Wilkes Booth
4. John Dalton
5. Sir John Everett Millais
6. Johann Wolfgang Amadeus Mozart
7. John L. Lewis
8. Ian Fleming
9. John Keats
10. Jan Vermeer

Crypto-Johns (p. 170)

1. "Idealism increases in direct proportion to one's distance from the problem." — John Galsworthy, English writer
2. "There are lots of people who can't think seriously without injuring their minds." — John Jay Chapman, American writer
3. "You don't have to suffer to be a poet. Adolescence is suffering enough for anyone." — John Ciardi, American poet
4. "A celebrity is a person who works hard all his life to become well known, then wears dark glasses to avoid being recognized." —Fred Allen (John F. Sullivan), American comedian
5. "There is hardly anything in the world that some men cannot make a little worse, and sell a little cheaper." — John Ruskin, British writer and art critic

Name That John (p. 171)

1. Johnny Cash
2. John Glenn
3. Jean-Pierre Rampal
4. Johnny Mathis
5. Jack Kemp

Crossword Puzzle 1 (p. 172)

Crossword Puzzle 2 (p. 174)

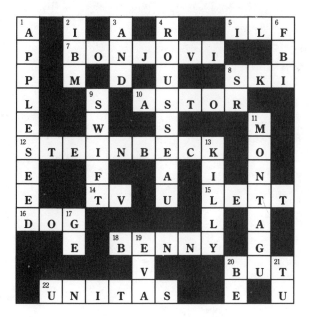

MORE JOHN TRIVIA! Answers

Scrambled Johns (p. 176)

1. Ivan Lendl
2. Jackie Robinson
3. Jackie Stewart
4. Johnny Unitas
5. John Adams
6. Ivan the Terrible
7. John L. Lewis
8. John Dewey
9. Jean Paul Getty
10. Hans Holbein
11. John Belushi
12. John Dryden
13. Evan Hunter
14. Jack London
15. Johann Wolfgang Amadeus Mozart
16. Jean Pierre Rampal
17. Jean Baptiste Molière
18. Zane Grey
19. Sean Connery

How many other anagrams can you come up with using these or other famous John names? Can you come up with any fun ones using your own name?

Who Said That? (p. 177)

1. E
2. C
3. A
4. D
5. B
6. I
7. G
8. F
9. H

Trivia Quiz (p. 178)

1. John Adams, John C. Calhoun, Richard M. Johnson, John Tyler, John C. Breckinridge, Andrew Johnson, (John) Calvin Coolidge, John Nance Garner, Lyndon B. Johnson
2. John F. Kennedy
3. John Paul Jones
4. (John) Calvin Coolidge
5. John Wesley Weasel
6. John F. Enders
7. Howard Johnson
8. John Hancock, Jack Johnson, John Paul Jones ...
9. John Waters
10. Governor Winthrop chair

Crypto-Johns (p. 179)

1. "Daring ideas are like chessmen moved forward; they may be beaten, but they may start a winning game." — Johann Wolfgang von Goethe, German writer
2. " 'Tis not the drinking that is to be blamed, but the excess." —John Selden, English judge
3. "When a man is wrapped up in himself, he makes a pretty small package." — John Ruskin, English art critic
4. "Life is a tragedy for those who feel, and a comedy for those who think." — Jean de la Bruyère, French writer
5. "We must believe in luck. For how else can we explain the success of those we don't like." — Jean Cocteau, French writer, filmmaker

Crossword Puzzle (p. 180)

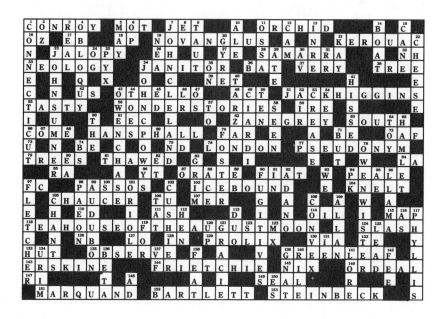

A Calendar of Johns

<table>
<tr><td rowspan="5">**JANUARY**</td><td>**1**
J(ohn) Edgar Hoover — 1895 - U.S. Dir. of FBI</td><td>**2**
John Bedford-Lloyd — U.S. actor</td><td>**3**
J(ohn) R.R. Tolkien — 1892 - Brit. writer *(The Hobbit)*</td></tr>
<tr><td>**8**
Hans Guido Von Bulow —1830 -Ger. musician, conductor

Hans Kindler — 1893 - Dutch conductor, musician</td><td>**9**
John Broadus Watson — 1878 - U.S. psychologist</td><td>**10**
John E.E. Dalberg, Lord Acton —1834 - Brit. historian

Johnnie Ray (John Alvin) — 1927 - U.S. singer</td></tr>
<tr><td>**15**
Jean-Baptiste Poquelin (Molière) —1622 - Fr. writer</td><td>**16**
John Carpenter — 1948 - U.S. director</td><td>**17**
John Sidney McCain, Jr. —1911 - U.S. admiral

James Earl Jones —1931 -U.S. actor</td></tr>
<tr><td>**22**
Ivan III — 1440 - Russ. ruler</td><td>**23**
John Logan —1923 -U.S. poet</td><td>**24**
John Belushi — 1949 -U.S. actor, comedian</td></tr>
<tr><td>**29**
John D. Rockefeller, Jr. — 1874 -U.S. philanthr.

John Forsythe — 1918 - U.S. actor</td><td>**30**
John Ireland — 1915 -Can. actor</td><td>**31**
Zane Grey — 1872 -U.S. writer

Jackie Robinson —1919 - U.S. baseball player</td></tr>
</table>

4	5	6	7
Giovanni Battista Pergolesi —1710 - Ital. composer **John McLaughlin** —1942 - Brit. singer, musician	**Jean-Pierre Aumont** — 1909 - Fr. actor, author **Juan Carlos I** — 1938 - King of Spain	**John Zachary DeLorean** — 1925 - U.S. auto exec., author	**Jean-Pierre Rampal** — 1922 - Fr. flutist **Jann Wenner** — 1947 - U.S. publisher *(Rolling Stone)*
11	**12** John	**13**	**14**
John A. Macdonald — 1815 - 1st Prime Minister of Canada	**Hancock** —1737 - U.S. statesman **John Singer Sargent** — 1856 - U.S. artist **Jack London** — 1876 -U.S. writer	**Jack Isidor Strauss** — 1900 - U.S. business exec. (Macy's)	**John Dos Passos** —1896 - U.S. writer
18	**19**	**20**	**21**
Janos Ferencsik —1907 - Hung. conductor **John Boorman** — 1933 - Brit. director	**Hans Hotter** — 1909 -Ger. Singer **John Emmet Raitt** —1917 - U.S. singer	**Johannes Vilhelm Jensen** 1873 - Danish writer **John Naber** —1956 -U.S. swimmer	**John Charles Fremont** — 1813 - U.S. explorer **Jack Nicklaus** — 1940 - U.S. golfer
25	**26**	**27**	**28**
Jack T. Snow — 1943 - U.S. football player	**John Quidor** — 1801 -U.S. artist **Jack De Manio** — 1914 - Brit. broadcast journalist	**Johann Wolfgang Amadeus Mozart** —1756 - Aus. composer	**Jackson Pollock** —1912 - U.S. artist

Additional January Birthdays:

12: John Winthrop — 1588 - Colonial governor

21: John Fitch — 1743 - U.S. inventor (steamship)

    John C. Breckinridge — 1821 - U.S. vice president

      Wolfman Jack (Robert Smith) — 1939 - U.S. DJ and TV personality

31: John O'Hara — 1905 - U.S. writer

193

F **E** **B** **R** **U** **A** **R** **Y**	**1** **John Ford** — 1895 - U.S. director	**2** **John Thomas Tudor** — 1954 -U.S. baseball pitcher	**3** **John Larry Jefferson** — 1956 - U.S. football player
	8 **John Ruskin** — 1819 - Brit. author, art critic **Jack Lemmon** — 1925 - U.S. actor	**9** **John Garnet Carter** — 1893 - U.S. inventor (miniature golf)	**10** **John F. Enders** — 1897 - U.S. physician **John Villiers Farrow** — 1906 - Australian dir.
	15 **John Barrymore** — 1882 - U.S. actor **Ian Ballantine** — 1916 - U.S. publisher	**16** **John P. McEnroe, Jr.** — 1959 - U.S. tennis player	**17** **Giovanni Pacini** — 1796 - Ital. composer
	22 **Sir John Mills** — 1908 - Brit. actor	**23** **Johannes Gutenberg** — 1400 - German inventor **Johnny Winter (John Dawson, III)** — 1944 - U.S. singer, musician	**24** **John Philip Holland** — 1841 - U.S. inventor 1st Navy submarine **John Vernon** — 1932 - Can. actor
	29 **"Pepper" Martin (John Leonard Roosevelt)** — 1904 - U.S. baseball player		

4	5	6	7
Johann Frederick Bottger — 1682 - Ger. chemist (developed Dresden china)	**John Boyd Dunlop** — 1840 - Scot. inventor **John Richmond Carradine** — 1906 - U.S. actor	**John Brown Gordon** — 1932 - U.S. general	**John Deere** —1804 - U.S. industrialist

11	12	13	14
John F. Fitzgerald (Honey Fitz) — 1863 - U.S. politician **John Mills** — 1889 - U.S. singer (Mills Brothers)	**John Llewellyn Lewis** — 1880 -U.S. labor union official	**John Hunter** — 1728 - Brit. surgeon	**Jack Benny (Benjamin Kubelsky)** — 1894 - U.S. comedian

18	19	20	21
Jack Palance — 1920 - U.S. actor **Johnny (Lewis) Hart** — 1931 - U.S. cartoonist **John Travolta** — 1954 - U.S. actor	**John Bubbles** — 1902 - U.S. dancer	**John Charles Daly, Jr.** — 1914 - U.S. TV host	**Cardinal John Henry Newman** — 1801 - Brit. theologian

25	26	27	28
John Foster Dulles — 1888 - U.S. Secretary of State	**Jackie Gleason** — 1916 - U.S. actor **Johnny Cash** — 1932 - U.S. singer, songwriter	**John Ernst Steinbeck** — 1902 - U.S. author	**Sir John Tenniel** — 1820 - Brit. cartoonist **John Alden Carpenter** — 1876 - U.S. composer **John Fahey** —1939 - U.S. musician

ADDITIONAL FEBRUARY BIRTHDAYS:

8: **John T. Williams** — 1932 -U.S. composer, conductor

9: **John A. Ziegler, Jr.** — 1934 - U.S. Pres. NHL

26: **Dr. John Kellogg** — 1852 - U.S. cereal inventor

M A R C H

1 Jean-Michel Folon — 1934 -Belg. artist	**2** John Irving —1942 - U.S. writer Jon Bon Jovi — 1962 - U.S. singer	**3** John Montgomery Ward — 1860 - U.S. baseball pitcher, pitched 18-inning shutout
8 (John) Douglass Wallop, III — 1920 - U.S. actor	**9** Jean-Baptiste Kleber — 1753 - French revolutionary John Duffield Curtis II — 1948 - U.S. baseball plater	**10** John McClosky — 1810 - 1st U.S. Cardinal
15 Ivan Allen, Jr. — 1911 - U.S. mayor of Atlanta John Gregson — 1919 - Brit. actor	**16** John Addison — 1920 - Brit. composer	**17** John Sebastian — 1944 - U.S. singer
22 John Frederick Kensett — 1816 - U.S. artist	**23** John Bartram — 1699 - U.S. botanist	**24** John Rock — 1890 - U.S. physician (devel. birth control pill) John Rogers Cox — 1915 - U.S. artist
29 John Tyler — 1790 - 10th U.S. president	**30** Sean O'Casey — 1880 - Irish dramatist John Allen Astin — 1930 - U.S. actor, director, writer	**31** Jack Johnson (John Arthur Johnson) — 1878 - U.S. boxer John Fowles — 1926 - Brit. author

4	5	6	7
John Garfield — 1913 · U.S. actor	**Jack Cassidy** — 1927 · U.S. actor, singer, dancer	**Johan Bojer** — 1872 · Norweg. writer	**Sir John Frederick William Herschel** — 1792 · Brit. astronomer **Ivan Lendl** — 1960 · Czech. tennis player
11	**12**	**13**	**14**
	Jack Kerouac — 1922 · U.S. writer (chronicler of "Beat Generation")	**Johann Rudolf Wyss** — 1782 · Swiss writer *(Swiss family Robinson)* **Juan Gris** — 1887 · Span. artist	**Johann Strauss, Sr.** — 1804 · Aus. composer, conductor **"Casey" Jones (John Luther Jones)** — 1864 · U.S. folk hero
18	**19**	**20**	**21**
John Caldwell Calhoun — 1782 · U.S. statesman **John Hoyer Updike** · 1932 · U.S. author	**John Joseph Sirica** — 1904 · U.S. judge **John Walter Kendall** — 1929 · U.S. scientist	**John Daniel Ehrlichman** —1925 · U.S. gov't. official	**Johann Sebastian Bach** — 1685 · Ger. composer **Jean Paul F. Richter** — 1763 · Ger. writer
25	**26**	**27**	**28**
John Winebrenner — 1797 · founder of Church of God **John W. Marriott, Jr.** — 1932 · U.S. restauranteur	**John Jorden Upchurch** — 1820 · U.S. labor leader **John Langshaw Austin** — 1911 · Brit. philosopher	**Giovanni Battista Grassi** — 1854 · Italian zoologist	**Johann Amos Comenius** — 1592 · Czech. theologian

ADDITIONAL MARCH BIRTHDAYS:

21: John D. Rockefeller III — 1906 · U.S. philanthropist

25: Elton John — 1947 · U.S. singer, songwriter

30: Ivan II (Ivan the Red) — 1326 · Russian ruler

1 Hans Conreid — 1915 - U.S. actor	**2** Giovanni Jacopo Casanova — 1725 - Ital. adventurer Hans Christian Andersen — 1805 - Dan. writer	**3** John Burroughs — 1837 - U.S. naturalist John Knight, III — 1945 - U.S. writer, editor
8 Juan Ponce de Leon — 1460 -Span. explorer John Raymond Gambling — 1950 - U.S. radio announcer	**9** John Bradley Gambling — 1897 - Brit.-Am. radio performer Jean-Paul Belmondo — 1933 - Fr. actor	**10** John Madden — 1936 - U.S. sportscaster
15 Johann Frederick Fasch — 1688 -Ger. composer	**16** John Millington Synge — 1871 -Irish author, dramatist	**17** John Piermont Morgan — 1837 - U.S. financier Jan Hammer — 1948 - Czech musician
22 John Buchanan — 1931 - Can. politician Jack Nicholson — 1937 - U.S. actor	**23** Jan Mayerowitz — 1913 - Ger. opera composer	**24** John Trumball — 1750 - U.S. poet, judge John Russell Pope — 1874 - U.S. architect
29 Johnny Laurence Miller — 1947 -U.S. golfer	**30** Johann F. Carl Gauss — 1777 -Ger. mathematician Johnny Horton — 1927 - U.S. country singer	

APRIL

4	**5**	**6**	**7**
Hans Richter — 1843 - Hung. conductor **John Cameron Swayze, Sr.** —1906 - U.S. journalist	**Jean Honore Fragonard —** 1732 - French artist	**Ivan Dixon —** 1931 - U.S. actor	**John Oates —** 1949 - U.S. singer (Hall & Oates)
11	**12**	**13**	**14**
Jean-Claude Servan-Schreiber — 1918 - Fr. journalist	**John Shaw Billings —** 1838 - U.S. librarian **John Landy** —1930 - Austral. track athlete	**John Hanson —** 1721 - 1st Pres. Continental Congress	**Sir (Arthur) John Gielgud —** 1904 - Brit. actor, director, producer
18	**19**	**20**	**21**
John E. Davis — 1913 - U.S. politician	**Jack Pardee —** 1936 - U.S. football player	**John Paul Stevens —** 1920 - Supreme Court Justice	**John Muir —** 1838 - U.S. naturalist **J(ack) W(alter) Lambert —** 1917 - Brit. critic
25	**26**	**27**	**28**
Johann Cruyff — 1947 - Dutch soccer player	**John James Audubon —** 1785 - U.S. artist	**Jack Klugman —** 1922 - U.S. actor	**John Jacob Niles** — 1892 - U.S. composer

ADDITIONAL APRIL BIRTHDAYS:

2: Jack Webb —1920 - U.S. actor, producer

8: John Gavin —1932 - U.S. actor, diplomat

24: John Williams — 1941 - Australian musician (Sky)

30: John Crowe Ransome — 1888 - U.S. writer

M A Y

1	2	3
Jack Parr - 1918 - U.S. entertainer	**John Galt** — 1779 - Scot. writer **John Neville** — 1925 - Brit. actor	**Jack La Rue** — 1902 - U.S. actor
8	9	10
Jean Henri Dunant — 1828 - Swiss founder of Red Cross **John Warne Gates** — 1855 -U.S. financier	**John Brown** — 1800 - U.S. abolitionist	**John Sherman** — 1823 - U.S. statesman
15	16	17
John F. Gordon — 1900 - U.S. auto executive **Jasper Johns** — 1930 - U.S. artist	**Jan Kiepura** — 1902 - Pol.-Am. singer **Johannes Georg Bednorz** — 1950 - Ger. scientist	**John Penn** — 1741 - U.S. signer of Decl. of Indep. **John Joseph Phelan** — 1931 - U.S. ch. exec. NY Stock Exch.
22	23	24
Janos Kadar — 1912 - Hung. communist leader	**John Bardeen** — 1908 - U.S. physicist, inventor of transistor **John Newcombe** — 1944 - Austral. tennis player	**Jan Christian Smuts** — 1870 - Prime Minister of South Africa
29	30	31
John Fitzgerald Kennedy — 1917 - 35th U.S. President	**Giovanni Gentile** — 1875 - Ital. philosopher	**Fred Allen (John F. Sullivan)** —1894 - U.S. comedian **Johnny Paycheck** — 1941 - U.S. singer

4	5	6	7
John Watson — 1946 - Irish auto racer	**John Batterson Stetson** — 1830 - U.S. hat manufacturer	**John Tinney McCutcheon** — 1870 - U.S. journalist	**Johannes Brahms** — 1833 - Ger. composer, pianist **Johnny Unitas** — 1933 - U.S. football player
11	**12**	**13**	**14**
John Shaw Billings — 1898 - U.S. editor	**John Paul Bucyk** — 1935 - Can. hockey player	**John McArthur** — 1823 - U.S. architect **John H. Roseboro** — 1933 - U.S. baseball player	**Jack Bruce** —1943 - Scot. musician
18	**19**	**20**	**21**
Pope John Paul II (Karol Jozef Wojtyla) — 1920 - Polish Pope **Jack Whitaker** — 1924 - U.S. sportscaster	**Johns Hopkins** — 1795 - U.S. merchant, philanthropist	**John Stuart Mill** — 1806 - Brit. philosopher	**John Frederick Peto** — 1854 - U.S. artist **Cardinal Giovanni Benelli** — 1921 - Ital. religious leader
25	**26**	**27**	**28**
John Raleigh Mott — 1865 - U.S. Nobel Peace Prize **John Gregory Dunne** — 1932 - U.S. writer	**John Wayne (Marion Morrison)** — 1907 - U.S. actor	**John Cheever** — 1912 - U.S. writer **John Barth** — 1930 - U.S. writer	**Jean Louis Agassiz** — 1807 - Swiss-Am. naturalist **Ian Lancaster Fleming** — 1908 - Brit. writer

ADDITIONAL MAY BIRTHDAYS

18: Reggie Jackson — 1946 - U.S. baseball player

25: Ian Murray McKellan — 1939 - British actor, director

28: John Birch — 1918 - U.S. spy

John Fogerty — 1945 - U.S. singer (Credence Clearwater Revival)

J U N E

1	2	3
John Masefield — 1878 - Brit. poet laureate **John Drinkwater** — 1882 - Brit. writer	**Johnny Weissmuller —** 1904 - U.S. swimmer, actor	**Johan Barthold Jongkind** — 1819 - Dutch artist **Ian Hunter** — 1946 - Brit. singer, musician
8	**9**	**10**
Sir John Everett Millais — 1829 - Brit. artist **John W. Campbell** — 1910 - U.S. science fiction writer, editor	**John Howard Payne** — 1791 -U.S. singer, wrote "Home, Sweet Home" **Johnny Ace** —1929 - U.S. singer	**Jean Lesage** — 1912 - Can. statesman **John Gianelli** — 1950 - U.S. basketball player
15	**16**	**17** John
Waylon Jennings — 1937 - U.S. singer **Johnny Halliday** — 1943 - Fr. singer	**Jack Albertson —** 1910 - U.S. actor **Juan Velasco Alvarado** — 1910 - Former President of Peru	**Wesley** —1703 - Brit. theologian, founder of Methodism **John Richard Hersey** — 1914 - U.S. writer
22	**23**	**24**
John Joseph Dempsey — 1879 - U.S. statesman	**Jean-Marie Lucienpierre Anouilh** — 1910 - Fr. dramatist	**John Cabot** — 1450 - Ital. explorer **Jack Dempsey** — 1895 - U.S. boxer
29	**30**	
J(ohn) Q(uincy) A(dams) Ward — 1830 - U.S. sculptor	**Juan Bosch** —1909 - Dom. writer, politician	

4 John **Blythe Drew Barrymore, Jr.** — 1932 - U.S. actor **John Francis McNamara** — 1932 - U.S. baseball manager	**5** **John Couch Adams** — 1819 - Brit. astronomer **John Maynard Keynes** — 1883 - Brit. economist	**6** **John Trumball** — 1756 - U.S. painter	**7** **John Strickland Goodall** — 1908 - Brit. artist
11 **John Constable** — 1776 - Brit. artist **Jackie Stewart** — 1939 - Scot. race car driver	**12** **John Augustus Roebling** — 1806 - U.S. engineer, pioneered suspension bridges	**13** **Ian Hunter** — 1900 - S. Afr. actor, screenwriter **John W. Joanis** — 1918 - U.S. founder Sentry Ins. Co.	**14** **John Bartlett** — 1820 - U.S. lexicographer - *Bartlett's Familiar Quotations*
18 **Ian Carmichael** — 1920 - Brit. actor **John D(avis) Rockefeller, IV** — 1937 - U.S. politician	**19** **Sir John Barrow** — 1764 - Brit. geographer, founded Royal Geographical Society	**20** **John Aloysius Costello** — 1891 - Irish Prime Minister **John A. Ogrodnick** — 1959 - Can. hockey player	**21** **Jean-Paul Sartre** — 1905 - Fr. philosopher
25 **John (Arthur) Chapman** — 1900 - U.S. drama critic **John Richard Briley** — 1925 - U.S. screenwriter	**26** **John Langdon** — 1741 - U.S. politician - 1st pro tem. president	**27** **Juan Terry Trippe** — 1899 - U.S. founder of Pan Am Airlines	**28** **Jean-Jacques Rousseau** — 1712 - Fr. philosopher **John Herbert Dillinger** — 1902 - U.S. criminal

ADDITIONAL JUNE BIRTHDAYS:

5: John Carlos — 1945 - U.S. track athlete

24: John the Baptist, feast day

John Anthony Ciardi — 1916 - U.S. poet, "Unofficial NJ poet laureate"

J**U****L****Y**	**1** **Jean Marie Lurcat** — 1892 - Fr. artist	**2** **(Jean-) Rene Lacoste** — 1905 - Fr. tennis player **John Joseph Ricardo** — 1924 - U.S. auto exec.	**3** **John Singleton Copley** — 1733 - U.S. artist **John Mason Brown** — 1900 - U.S. critic, lecturer
	8 **Jean de LaFontaine** — 1621 - Fr. writer **John D. Rockefeller** — 1839 - U.S. indus., philanthropist	**9** **Jean Cassou** — 1879 - Fr. author, critic	**10** **John Calvin** —1509 - Fr. theologian, reformer **John Gilbert** — 1897 - U.S. actor
	15 **Jan-Michael Vincent** — 1944 - U.S. actor	**16** **Jean-Baptiste Camille Corot** — 1796 - Fr. painter	**17** **John Jacob Astor** — 1763 - U.S. financier
	22 **Jack Glassock** — 1859 - U.S. baseball player **Hans Rosbaud** — 1895 - Aus. conductor	**23** **Jan Troell** — 1931 - Swedish director	**24** **John D(ann) MacDonald** — 1916 -U.S. writer **Jack O'Callahan** — 1957 - U.S. Olympic hockey player
	29 **John Sargent Pillsbury** — 1828 - U.S. manufacturer, politician	**30** **John A. Carroll** — 1901 - U.S. politician	**31** **John Ericsson** — 1803 - U.S. engineer **Jean Panquette** — 1848 - Fr. composer

4	5	6	7
Jean François Blanchard — 1763 - Fr. balloonist **(John) Calvin Coolidge** — 1872 - 30th U.S. President	**Jan Kubelik** — 1880 - Czech musician **Jean Cocteau** — 1889 - Fr. writer, director	**John Paul Jones** — 1747 - U.S. naval hero	**Gian-Carlo Menotti** — 1911 - U.S. operatic composer **Jean Casadesus** — 1927 - Fr. musician
11	**12**	**13**	**14**
John Quincy Adams — 1767 -6th U.S. President **John Wanamaker** — 1838 - U.S. merchant	**John Crosby** — 1926 - U.S. conductor	**John Clare** — 1793 - Brit. poet **Jack French Kemp** — 1935 -U.S. congressman	**Owen Wister** — 1860 - U.S. writer **John William Chancellor** — 1927 - U.S. TV journalist
18	**19**	**20**	**21**
John Herschel Glenn, Jr. — 1921 - U.S. astronaut, senator	**Johann Jakob Bodmer** — 1698 - Swiss poet **John Purroy Mitchel** — 1879 - U.S. mayor of New York	**Baron John Charles Walsham Reith** — 1889 - Brit. "Father of BBC"	**John Joseph Evers** — 1881 - U.S. baseball player **John B. Keane** — 1928 - Irish writer
25	**26**	**27**	**28**
Jack Gilford —1913 - U.S. actor	**John Field** — 1782 - Irish pianist, composer	**Hans Haug** — 1900 - Swiss opera composer	**(John) Selwyn Brooke Lloyd** — 1904 - Brit. politician

ADDITIONAL JULY BIRTHDAYS:

21: Jonathan Miller — 1934 - British actor

AUGUST

1	2	3
Jack Kramer — 1921 - U.S. tennis player	**John French Sloan** —1871 - U.S. artist **Jack Leonard Warner** —1892 - U.S. film exec.	**John Thomas Scopes** — 1900 - U.S. teacher **John Gunther** — 1910 - U.S. writer, journalist
8	**9**	**10**
John C. Culver — 1932 - U.S. politician	**John Dryden** — 1631 - Brit. poet, dramatist	**Jack Haley** — 1900 - U.S. actor - Tin Man in *Wizard of Oz*
15	**16**	**17**
John Lynch —1917 - Irish Prime Minister	**Jean de La Bruyère** —1645 -Fr. writer, philosopher	**John Sobieski III** — 1624 - Polish king **Sean Penn** — 1960 - U.S. actor
22	**23**	**24**
Jean François Ducis —1733 - Fr. writer **John Lee Hooker** —1917 - U.S. singer	**Ian Fraser** — 1933 - Brit. composer, conductor	**J(ohn) Burke Wilkinson** — 1913 - U.S. writer
29	**30**	**31**
John Locke —1632 - Brit. philosopher **Jack R. Thornell** —1939 - U.S. photog.	**John Phillips** — 1935 - U.S. singer, Mamas & the Papas **Jean-Claude Killy** — 1943 - Fr. skier	**Giovanni Verga** — 1840 - Ital. writer **Jean Marc Beliveau** — 1931 -Can. hockey player

4	**5**	**6**	**7**
John Riggins — 1949 - U.S. football player **Jack Brand** — 1953 - Can. soccer player	**John Eliot** — 1604 - U.S. clergyman **John Huston** — 1906 - U.S. director	**John Ewart Wallace Sterling** — 1906 - U.S. President Stanford Univ. for 2 decades	**Johann Valentin Andrae** — 1586 - Ger. pastor, originated Rosicrucian legend
11	**12**	**13**	**14**
Ian Charleson — 1949 - Scot. actor	**John Derek** — 1926 - U.S. actor	**John Ireland** — 1879 - Brit. composer **John Logie Baird** — 1888 - Scot. inventor	**Hans Christian Oersted** — 1777 - Dan. physicist **John Galsworthy** — 1867 - Brit. writer
18	**19**	**20**	**21**
Lord John Russell — 1792 - Brit. Prime minister	**Johnny Nash** — 1940 - U.S. singer	**Jack Teagarden** — 1905 - U.S. jazz musician	**Jean-Baptiste Greuze** — 1725 - French artist **Jack Weston** — 1915 - U.S. actor
25	**26**	**27**	**28**
Ivan IV (Ivan the Terrible — 1530 - Russian Czar **Sean Connery** — 1930 - Scot. actor	**John Wilkes Booth** — 1838 - U.S. actor, assassin **Sir John Buchan** — 1875 - Scot. Gov.-Gen. of Canada	**Lyndon B. Johnson** — 1908 - 36th U.S. Pres. **John Lloyd** — 1954 - Brit. tennis player	**Johann Wolfgang von Goethe** —1749 - Ger. writer **Sir John Betjeman** — 1906 - Brit. poet

ADDITIONAL AUGUST BIRTHDAYS:

5: John Saxon — 1935 - U.S. actor

14: John Ringling North — 1903 -U.S. circus own.

25: Sir Hans Krebs — 1900 - British scientist

29: Jean Lafitte — 1780 - French pirate

29: Jean A.D. Ingres — 1780 - French painter

29: Michael Jackson — 1958 - U.S. singer

S E P T E M B E R	**1** Johann Pachelbel — 1653 - Ger. composer	**2** Hiram Johnson — 1866 - U.S. politician	**3** Johann Christian Bach — 1735 - Ger. composer John Humphrey Noyes — 1811 -U.S. founder of Oneida Community
	8 Jean-Louis Barrault — 1910 - Fr. actor, director	**9** John Grey Gorton — 1911 - Austral. prime minister John Anthony Curry — 1949 -Brit. Olympic gold skater	**10** Sir John Sloane — 1753 - Brit. architect John Entwistle — 1944 - Brit. musician (The Who)
	15 Jean Renoir — 1894 - Fr. director, screenwriter Jackie Cooper — 1922 - U.S. actor	**16** Hans Arp — 1887 - Fr. sculptor John Knowles — 1926 - U.S. writer	**17** John Williard Marriott — 1900 - U.S. restauranteur John Ritter — (Jonathan Southworth) — 1948 - U.S. actor
	22 John Houseman — 1902 - U.S. producer, director, actor	**23** John Lomax — 1870 - U.S. folklorist John Boyd Orr — 1880 - Scot. physician, Nobel Peace Prize	**24** John Marshall — 1755 - U.S. chief justice John Watts Young — 1930 - U.S. astronaut
	29 Jean-Luc Ponty — 1942 - Fr. composer, violinist	**30** Hans Geiger — 1882 - Ger. physicist Johnny Mathis — 1935 - U.S. singer Jean-Marie Lehn — 1939 - Fr. chemist	

4	5	6	7
Ivan Illich — 1926 - U.S. educator John Vanbiesbrouck — 1963 - U.S. hockey player	John Milton Cage, Jr. — 1912 - U.S. composer Jack Joseph Valenti — 1921 - U.S. Pres. Motion Picture Assoc.	John Dalton — 1766 - Brit. scientist	J(ohn) P(iermont) Morgan, Jr. —1867 - U.S. philanthropist

11	12	13	14
Jack Gardiner Richards — 1864 - U.S. politician	Jesse Owens — 1913 - U.S. athlete Ian Holm — 1931 - Brit. actor	John Joseph Pershing — 1860 - U.S. general	Ivan Petrovich Pavlov — 1849 - Rus. physiologist

18	19	20 John	21
Jean Bernard Foucault — 1819 - Fr. physicist Jack Warden — 1920 - U.S. actor	Jay Randolph — (Jennings Randolph) — 1934 - U.S. sportscaster	Murray Anderson — 1886 -Brit. director John Philip William Dankworth —1927 - Brit. composer	Hans Hartung — 1863 - Fr. artist

25	26	27	28
Jean-Philippe Rameau — 1683 - Fr. composer Ian Tyson — 1933 - Can. singer, songwriter (Ian and Sylvia)	Johnny Appleseed — 1774 - U.S. folk hero Jean Gericault — 1791 - Fr. artist	John Fischetti — 1916 - U.S. cartoonist Shaun Cassidy — 1958 - U.S. actor, singer	Jack Bernard Hofsiss — 1950 - U.S. director

ADDITIONAL SEPTEMBER BIRTHDAYS:

9: **John Hall Wheelock** — 1886 - U.S. poet

26: **(John William) "Trane" Coltraine** — 1926 - U.S. jazz musician

Jack LaLanne — 1914 - U.S. physical fitness expert

1 **John Brown Russwurm** — 1799 - U.S. journalist	**2** **John Ross** — 1790 - U.S. Indian Chief	**3** **John Gorrie** —1803 - U.S. inventor
8 **Juan Peron** —1895 - President of Argentina **Jesse Jackson** — 1941 - U.S. civil rts. leader	**9** **John Winston Lennon** — 1940 - Brit. singer, songwriter **Jackson Browne** — 1950 - U.S. singer, songwriter	**10** **Jean-Antoine Watteau** — 1684 - Fr. artist **John Mohler Studebaker** —1833 - U.S. auto manufacturer
15 **John L. Sullivan** — 1858 - U.S. boxer **Evan Hunter (Salvatore Lombino)** — 1926 - U.S. writer	**16** **John Bagnell Bury** — 1681 - Irish historian	**17** **John Wilkes** — 1727 - Brit. reformer **John Marley** — 1916 - U.S. actor
22 **Johnny Beckman** — 1895 - U.S. basketball player	**23** **Johnny Carson** — 1925 - U.S. TV host, entertainer	**24** **John Sartain** — 1808 - U.S. engraver **Juan Marichal** — 1937 - Dominican baseball player
29 **Jean Giraudoux** — 1882 - Fr. writer **Zoot Sims (John Haley)** — 1925 - U.S. jazz musician	**30** **Jan Vermeer** — 1632 - Dutch artist **John Adams** — 1735 - 2nd U.S. President	**31** **John Keats** — 1795 - Brit. poet **John Candy** —1950 - Can. actor, comedian

OCTOBER

4 Jean-François Millet —1814 - Fr. artist	**5** Jonathan Edwards —1703 - U.S. theologian John Erskine — 1879 - U.S. educator	**6** John Willis Griffiths —1809 - U.S. architect	**7** Jack Mulhall — 1894 - U.S. actor Jonathan Jones — 1911 - U.S. jazz drummer
11 Hans Kelsen — 1881 - Czech writer, educator	**12** Jonathan Trumball —1710 - U.S. judge, politician	**13** John Rogers Commons — 1862 -U.S. historian, economist John Herbert (Brundage) —1926 - Can. playwright	**14** John Wesley Dean — 1938 - U.S. lawyer - Richard Nixon's counsel in Watergate
18 Jean-Jacques Regis de Cambacères — 1753 - Fr. advisor to Napoleon John Boles — 1895 - U.S. actor	**19** Jack Northman Anderson — 1922 - U.S. journalist John Lithgow — 1945 - U.S. actor	**20** John Dewey — 1859 - U.S. philosopher, educator	**21** "Dizzy" Gillespie (John Birks) — 1917 - U.S. jazz trumpeter
25 Johann Strauss, Jr. — 1825 - Aus. composer Jon Anderson — 1944 - U.S. singer, musician (Yes)	**26** Jackie Coogan — 1914 - U.S. actor John Arden —1930 - Brit. playwright	**27** John Cleese — 1939 - Brit. actor, writer	**28** Jonas Edward Salk — 1914 - U.S. physician, researcher

ADDITIONAL OCTOBER BIRTHDAYS:

5: John Addington Symonds — 1840 - British historian, translator, poet

8: John Clarke — 1609 - British founder of Rhode Island

15: John Kenneth Galbraith — 1908 - U.S. economist

17: John Paul I — 1912 - Italian Pope (for only 34 days!)

NOVEMBER

1	2	3
John Secondari — 1919 - U.S. TV producer	**Johnny Vander Meer** — 1914 - U.S. baseball player	**John Barry** — 1933 - Brit. composer
8	9	10
John Allen Denny — 1952 - U.S. baseball pitcher	**Ivan Surgeevich Turgenev** — 1818 - Rus. writer **John H. Holmes** — 1879 - U.S. rel. ref.	**J(ohn) P. Marquand** — 1893 - U.S. writer **Johnny Marks** — 1909 - U.S. songwriter
15 **Johann Casper Lavater** — 1741 -Swiss writer, theologian **John Coleman** — 1935 - U.S. weatherman, *Good Morning America*	16 **Jean le Rond d'Alembert** — 1717 - French mathematician, philosopher	17 **Jack Lescoulie** — 1917 - U.S. TV personality
22 **John Nance Garner** — 1868 - U.S. vice president	23 **John Forkum Dehner** — 1915 - U.S. actor	24 **John Vliet Lindsay** — 1921 - U.S. mayor NYC
29 **John Ambrose Fleming** — 1849 - Brit. physicist **John Gary** — 1932 - U.S. singer	30 **Jonathan Swift** — 1667 - Irish satirist, clergyman	

4	**5**	**6**	**7**
John Allen — 1810 - U.S. dentist, invented false teeth **John Cecil Holm** — 1904 - U.S. actor, playwright	**Hans Sachs** —1494 - Ger. writer, composer **John McGiver** — 1913 - U.S. actor	**John Philip Sousa** — 1854 - U.S. composer, conductor	**Johnny Rivers** — 1942 - U.S. singer
11	**12**	**13**	**14**
Jonathan Winters — 1925 - U.S. comedian	**Jack Oakie** — 1903 - U.S. actor	**Jack Elam** — 1916 - U.S. actor	**John Stewart Curry** — 1897 -U.S. artist **Johnny Desmond** — 1921 - U.S. singer, actor
18	**19**	**20**	**21**
Johnny Mercer — 1909 - U.S. singer, songwriter	**John Francis Welch** — 1935 -U.S. chairman General Electric	**Jay (John William, Jr.) Johnstone** — 1945 - U.S. baseball player	**Voltaire (Jean-François Marie Arouet)** — 1694 - French writer, philosopher
25	**26**	**27**	**28**
John Larroquette — 1947 - U.S. actor **John Fitzgerald Kennedy Jr.** — 1960 - son of U.S. President	**John Harvard** — 1607 - Brit. clergyman **John McVie** —1946 - U.S. singer (Fleetwood Mac)	**John Victor McNally** — 1904 - U.S. football player	**John Bunyan** — 1628 - Brit. minister, writer **Jean-Baptiste Lully** — 1632 - Fr. composer

ADDITIONAL NOVEMBER BIRTHDAYS:

10: **Johann von Schiller** — 1759 - German writer

25: **John XXIII** — 1881 - Italian Pope

29: **John Brumwell Mayall** — 1933 - U.S. jazz musician

1 **Johnny Johnston** — 1915 - U.S. actor **John Densmore** — 1945 - U.S. singer (The Doors)	**2** **Sir John Barbirolli** — 1899 - Brit. conductor	**3** **Jean Luc Godard** - 1930 - Fr. director **"Ozzie" (John) Osborne** — 1949 - Brit. singer
8 **Jean Sibelius** — 1865 - Finn. composer	**9 John Milton** —Brit. poet **Redd Foxx (John Elroy Sanford)** — 1922 - U.S. comedian **John Cassavetes** — 1929 - U.S. actor, dir.	**10** **John Selden** — 1584 - Brit. judge **Johnny Rodriguez** — 1951 - U.S. musician
15 **J(ean) Paul Getty** — 1892 - U.S. oil billionaire	**16** **John W. Fox, Jr.** — 1863 - U.S. writer **John Edward Jacob** — 1934 - U.S. pres. Natl. Urban League	**17** **John Greenleaf Whittier** — 1807 - U.S. poet, essayist
22 **John Crome** — 1768 - Brit. artist	**23** **John Marin** —1872 - U.S. artist	**24** **John Lackland** — 1167 - King of England **John Ramon Jimenez** — 1881 - Sp. poet
29 **Andrew Johnson** — 1808 - 17th U.S. Pres. **Jon Voight** — 1938 - U.S. actor	**30** **Jack Lord** — 1930 - U.S. actor	**31** **John Wycliffe** — 1320 - Brit. theologian **John Denver** — 1943 - U.S. singer, songwriter

DECEMBER

4	5	6	7
John Cotton — 1584 - Amer. rel. ldr. **John Calvin Portman** — 1924 - U.S. architect	**Jack Conroy** — 1899 - U.S. writer	**Jocko Conlan (John Bertrand Conlan)** — 1899 - U.S. baseball umpire	**Giovanni Lorenzo Bernini** — 1598 - Ital. sculptor **Johnny Lee Bench** — 1947 -U.S. baseball player
11	**12**	**13**	**14**
John Moors Cabot — 1901 - U.S. diplomat **Jean-Louis Xavier Trintignant** —1930 - Fr. actor	**John Jay** — 1745 - First U.S. chief justice	**John Davidson** — 1941 - U.S. singer, actor	**John Mercer Langston** — 1829 - First U.S. black in public office
18	**19**	**20**	**21**
Jack Bascom Brooks — 1922 - U.S. congressman	**Jean Genet** — 1910 - Fr. playwright	**John Fletcher** — 1579 - Brit. writer	**John William McCormack** —1891 - U.S. opera singer
25	**26**	**27**	**28**
Johann Adam Hiller — 1728 - Pruss. composer **Jack Warren Lowe** — 1917 - U.S. musician	**(John) Frank Broyles** — 1924 - U.S. football player, sportscaster	**Giovanni Palestrina** — 1525 - Ital. composer **Johannes Kepler** — 1571 - Ger. astronomer	**John Fellows Akers** — 1934 -U.S. Chairman IBM

ADDITIONAL DECEMBER BIRTHDAYS:

27: John the Apostle (feast day)

John Amos — 1942 - U.S. actor

JOHN HOMETOWNS

Adams, John
Braintree, Massachusetts

Adams, John Quincy
Braintree, Massachusetts

Agassiz, Jean Louis
Motier, Switzerland

Akers, John Fellows
Boston, Massachusetts

Alcock, John W.
Manchester, England

Alden, John
England

Allen, Fred
Cambridge, Massachusetts

Andersen, Hans Christian
Odense, Denmark

Anouilh, Jean
Bordeaux, France

Appleseed, Johnny
Leominster, Massachusetts

Arbuthnot, John
Arbuthnot, Scotland

Ashbery, John
Rochester, New York

Astor, John Jacob
Waldorf, Germany

Audubon, John James
Les Cayes, Santo Domingo
(now Haiti)

Bach, Johann Sebastian
Eisenach, Germany

Baird, John Logie
Helensburgh, Scotland

Barrymore, John
Philadelphia, Pennsylvania

Bednorz, Johannes
Neu Kirchen, Nordrhein-
Westfalen, W. Germany

Bellini, Giovanni,
Venice, Italy

Belushi, John
Chicago, Illinois

Bench, Johnny
Oklahoma City, Oklahoma

Benny, Jack
Waukegan, Illinois

Bernini, Gian Lorenzo
Naples, Italy

Boccaccio, Giovanni
Paris, France

Bon Jovi, Jon
Sayreville, New Jersey

Brahms, Johannes
Hamburg, Germany

Brown, John
Torrington, Connecticut

Cabot, John
Genoa, Italy

Cage, John
Los Angeles, California

Calvin, John
Noyon, France

Campbell, John W.
Newark, New Jersey

Carlos, Juan I
Rome, Italy

Carson, Johnny
Corning, Iowa

Casanova, Giovanni
Venice, Italy

Cash, Johnny
Kingsland, Arkansas

Connery, Sean
Edinburgh, Scotland

Constable, John
East Bergholt, Suffolk,
England

Coogan, Jackie
Los Angeles, California

Coolidge, Calvin
Plymouth, Vermont

Copley, John Singleton
Boston, Massachusetts

Corot, Jean-Baptiste-Camille
Paris, France

Dalton, John
Eaglesfield, Cumberland,
England

216

Deere, John
Rutland, Vermont

Dempsey, Jack
Manassa, Colorado

Denver, John
Roswell, New Mexico

Donne, John
London, England

Dryden, John
Aldwinkle,
Northhamptonshire, England

Dunlop, John B.
Scotland

Fitch, John
Hartford, Connecticut

Fleming, Ian Lancaster
London, England

Ford, John
Cape Elizabeth, Maine

Forsythe, John
Penn's Grove, New Jersey

Foxx, Redd
St. Louis, Missouri

Fremont, John Charles
Savannah, Georgia

Galbraith, John Kenneth
Iona Station, Ontario, Canada

Gambling, John Alfred
New York City

Gambling, John Bradley
Norwich, England

Gambling, John Raymond
New York City

Gates, John Warne
Turner Junction, Illinois

Gauss, Carl Friedrich
Brunswick, Germany

Getty, J. Paul
Minneapolis, Minnesota

Gleason, Jackie
Brooklyn, New York

Glenn, John
Cambridge, Ohio

Goethe, Johann Wolfgang von
Frankfurt, Germany

Grey, Zane
Zanesville, Ohio

Gutenberg, Johann
Mainz, Germany

Hancock, John
Braintree, Massachusetts

Hart, Johnny
Endicott, New York

Holbein, Hans, the Younger
Augsburg, Germany

Holliday, John Henry
Griffin, Georgia

Hoover, J. Edgar
Washington, D.C.

Houseman, John
Bucharest, Rumania

Hunter, Evan
New York, New York

Huston, John
Nevada, Missouri

Ivan IV of Russia
Kolomenskoye, near Moscow,
Russia

Jackson, Jesse Louis
Greenville, South Carolina

Jackson, Michael Joseph
Gary, Indiana

Jackson, Reggie
Wyncote, Pennsylvania

Jennings, Waylon
Littlefield, Texas

Saint John the Apostle
Galillee

John the Baptist
Judea

Pope John Paul II
Wadowice, Poland

John, Elton
Pinner, England

Johns, Jasper
Augusta, Georgia

Johnson, Andrew
Raleigh, North Carolina

Johnson, Jack
Galveston, Texas

Johnson, Lyndon B.
Stonewall, Texas

Jonathan
Israel

Jones, James Earl
Arkabutla, Mississippi

Jones, John Paul
Kirkcudbrightshire, Scotland

Keats, John
London, England

Kemp, Jack French
Los Angeles, California

Kennedy, John F.
Brookline, Massachusetts

Kepler, Johannes
Weil der Stadt, Wurttemberg,
Germany

Keynes, John Maynard
Cambridge, England

Killy, Jean-Claude
Saint-Cloud, Paris, France

Kramer, Jack
Las Vegas, Nevada

Krebs, Hans Adolf
Hildesheim, Germany

Lackland, John
Oxford, England

Lafitte, Jean
France

Langdon, John
Portsmouth, New Hampshire

Lehn, Jean-Marie
Rosheim, France

Lemmon, Jack
Boston, Massachusetts

Lendl, Ivan
Ostrava, Czechoslovakia

Lennon, John
Liverpool, England

Lewis, John L.
near Lucas, Iowa

Locke, John
Wrington, England

London, Jack
San Francisco, California

Marichal, Juan
Laguna Verde, Dominican
Republic

Marshall, John
Germantown (now Midland),
Virginia

Masefield, John
Ledbury, England

Mason, Jackie
Sheboygan, Wisconsin

Mathis, Johnny
San Francisco, California

McEnroe, John
Wiesbaden, Germany

Menotti, Gian-Carlo
Cadegliano, Italy

Mill, John Stuart
London, England

Millais, Sir John Everett
Southhampton, Hampshire,
England

Milton, John
London, England

Molière
Paris, France

Morgan, John Pierpont
Hartford, Connecticut

**Mozart, Johann Wolfgang
Amadeus**
Salzburg, Austria

Muir, John
Dunbar, Scotland

Nicholson, Jack
Neptune, New Jersey

Nicklaus, Jack
Columbus, Ohio

Oates, John
New York City

O'Casey, Sean
Dublin, Ireland

Owens, Jesse
Danville, Alabama

Pavlov, Ivan Petrovich
Ryazan, Russia

Penn, Sean
Santa Monica, California

Peron, Juan Domingo
Province of Buenos Aires,
Argentina

Pollock, Jackson
Cody, Wyoming

Ponce de Leon, Juan
Tierra de Campos Palencia, Leon

Portman, John Calvin, Jr.
Walhalla, South Carolina

Rampal, Jean-Pierre
Marseilles, France

Robinson, Jackie
Cairo, Georgia

Rockefeller, John Davison
Richford, New York

Roebling, John A.
Muhlhausen, Germany

Rousseau, Jean-Jacques
Geneva, Switzerland

Ruskin, John
London, England

Russwurm, John B.
Port Antonio, Jamaica

Sachs, Hans
Nuremburg, Germany

Salk, Jonas Edward
New York City

Sargent, John Singer
Florence, Italy

Sartre, Jean-Paul
Paris, France

Scopes, John T.
Paducah, Kentucky

Sibelius, Jean
Hameenlinna, Finland

Sloan, John French
Lock Haven, Pennsylvania

Smith, John
Willoughby, Lincolnshire, England

Smuts, Jan Christiaan
Bovenplaats, near Riebeeck West, Cape Colony

Sousa, John Philip
Washington, D.C.

Steinbeck, John
Salinas, California

Stewart, Jackie
Milton, Dumbartonshire, Scotland

Strauss, Johann
Vienna, Austria

Swift, Jonathan
Dublin, Ireland

Thornell, Jack Randolph
Vicksburg, Mississippi

Travolta, John
Englewood, New Jersey

Tyler, John
Charles City, Virginia

Unitas, Johnny
Pittsburgh, Pennsylvania

Updike, John Hoyer
Shillington, Pennsylvania

Vander Meer, Johnny
Prospect Park, New Jersey

Vermeer, Jan
Delft, Netherlands

Voight, Jon
Yonkers, New York

Wanamaker, John
Philadephia, Pennsylvania

Watson, John B.
Greenville, South Carolina

Wayne, John
Winterset, Iowa

Weissmuller, Johnny
Windber, Pennsylvania

Welch, John Francis, Jr.
Peabody, Massachusetts

Wesley, John
Epworth, Lincolnshire, England

Williams, John
Flushing, New York

Winters, Jonathan
Dayton, Ohio

Winthrop, John
Suffolk, England

Wister, Owen
Germantown, Pennsylvania

Wolfman Jack
Brooklyn, New York

Wycliffe, John
Richmond, England

Zenger, John Peter
Germany

SELECTED BIBLIOGRAPHY

Hundreds of sources were consulted while gathering information for *JOHN, Your Name Is Famous*. For more information about the JOHN clan, and your favorite Johns, here are some of the most useful references:

Andersen, Christopher, *The Book of People* (Putnam, New York: 1981).

Allen, Maury, *Maury Allen Baseball's 100* (A&W Visual Lib., New York: 1981).

Asimov, Isaac, *Asimov's Biographical Encyclopedia of Science & Technology* (Doubleday, Garden City, NY: 1983).

Associated Press, *Sports Immortals* (Rutledge Books, Edison, NJ: 1972).

Auden & Kronenberger, 'The Viking Book of Aphorisms (Dorset Press, New York: 1981).

Bailey, Sandra, *Big Book of Baby Names* (HP Books, Tucson, AZ: 1982).

Bane, Michael, *Who's Who In Rock* (Dodd, Mead, New York: 1982).

Baring-Gould, William & Cecil, *Annotated Mother Goose* (Bramhall, New York: 1962).

Brewer, E. Cobham, *Brewer's Dictionary of Phrase and Fable* (Harper & Row, New York: 1970).

Brooks, Tim, *Complete Directory To Prime Time TV Stars* (Ballantine, New York: 1987).

Carruth, Gorton, ed., *American Facts and Dates* (Crowell, New York: 1966).

Ciardi, John. *A Browser's Dictionary* (Harper & Row, New York: 1980).

Conrad, Barnaby, *Famous Last Words* (Doubleday, Garden City, New York: 1961).

Contemporary Authors (Gale Research).

Contemporary Newsmakers (Gale Research).

Contemporary Theatre, Film & Television (Gale Research).

Current Biography (H.W. Wilson).

Dale, Steve, *All Time Favorite Movie Stars* (Publications Intl: 1986).

Dormann, Henry O., *The Speaker's Book of Quotations* (Fawcett Columbine, New York: 1987).

Dunkling & Gosling, *The New American Dictionary of First Names* (NAL, New York: 1983).

Encyclopedia Britannica.

Esquire Press, *Fifty Who Made the Difference* (Villard Books, New York: 1984).

Fadiman, Clifton. *The Little, Brown Book of Anecdotes* (Little Brown, Boston: 1985).

Frey, Alfred R., *Sobriquets and Nicknames* (Ticknor, Boston: 1888 — reprint Gale Research, Detroit: 1966).

Fullerton, Timothy T., *Triviata: A Comedium of Useless Information* (Hart, New York: 1975).

Funk, Wilfred, *Word Origins & Their Romantic Stories* (Bell Pub, New York: 1950).

Garrison, Webb, *How It Started* (Abingdon Press, New York: 1972).

Hart, Michael H., *The 100: A Ranking of the Most Influential Persons in History* (Hart Pub., New York: 1978).

Hauge & Kelly, *Nicknames* (Macmillan, New York: 1987).

Helander, Brock, *The Rock Who's Who* (Schirmer Books, New York: 1982).

Hirschhorn, Joel, *Rating the Movie Stars* (Beekman House, New York: 1983).

Hollander, *Great American Athletes of the 20th Century* (Random House, New York: 1972).

Jackson, Richard, *Popular Songs of 19th Century America* (Dover Pub, New York: 1976).

Jobes, Gertrude, *Dictionary of Mythology Folklore & Symbols* (Scarecrow, New York: 1962).

Kane, Joseph N., *Famous First Facts* (H.W. Wilson, New York: 1981).

Katz, Ephraim, *The Film Encyclopedia* (Perigee, New York: 1979).

Kunitz, Stanley & Howard Haycraft, *British Authors Before 1800* (H. W. Wilson, New York: 1952).

Lamparski, Richard, *Whatever Became of...* (Crown Publishers, New York).

Lax & Smith, *The Great Song Thesaurus* (Oxford U Press, New York: 1984).

Lieberman, Gerald F., *3500 Good Quotes for Speakers* (Doubleday, New York: 1983).

Lucaire, Ed., *Celebrity Book of Lists* (Stein & Day, New York: 1984).

Lucaire, Ed., *The Celebrity Book of Super Lists* (Stein & Day, New York: 1985).

Magill, Frank N., ed., *Cyclopedia of World Authors* (Harper & Row, New York: 1958).

Magill, Frank N., ed., *Masterplots* (Salem Press, New York: 1971).

McNeil, Alex, *Total Television* (Penguin, New York: 1984).

Morris, William & Mary, *Dictionary of Word & Phrase Origins* (Harper & Row, New York: 1962).

Murray, Peter and Linda, *Penguin Dictionary of Arts & Artists* (Penguin Books, New York: 1986).

Nelson, Randy F., *The Almanac of American Letters* (Kaufmann, Los Altos, CA: 1981).

New International Illustrated Encyclopedia of Art (Greystone Press, New York: 1968).

New York Times Biographical Service.

Nisenson, Samuel, *Dictionary of 1001 Famous People* (Lion Press, New York: 1966).

Nite, Norm N., *Rock On*, Vol. 1,2,3 (Harper & Row, New York: 1984).

Norman, Barry, *The Film Greats* (Watts, New York: 1985).

Nurnberg, Maxwell, *What to Name Your Baby* (Collier Books, New York: 1962).

Opic, Iona & Peter, ed., *The Oxford Dictionary of Nursery Rhymes* (Oxford U. Press, New York: 1962).

Oxford Dictionary of Quotations, 3rd edition (Oxford U. Press, New York: 1979).

Panati, Charles, *Browser's Book of Beginnings* (Houghton Mifflin, Boston: 1984).

Panati, Charles, *Extraordinary Origins of Everyday Things* (Harper & Row, New York: 1987).

Payton, Geoffrey, *Webster's Dictionary of Proper Names* (G&C Merriam, Springfield, MA: 1970).

Robertson, Patrick, *The Book of Firsts* (Clarkson, N. Potter, New York: 1974).

Roxon, Lillian, *Rock Encyclopedia* (Grosset & Dunlop, New York: 1969).

Sanders, Dennis, *The First of Everything* (Delacorte, New York: 1981).

Seldes, George, *The Great Quotations* (Citadel Press, Secaucus, NJ: 1983).

Shankle, George, *American Nicknames* (H. W., Wilson, New York: 1955).

Shipley, Joseph T., *Dictionary of Word Origins* (Philosophical Lib., New York: 1980).

Sifakais, Carl, *The Dictionary of Historic Nicknames* (Facts on File, New York: 1984).

Simpson, James, *Simpson's Contemporary Quotations* (Houghton Mifflin, Boston: 1988).

Something About the Author (Gale Research).

Stambler, Irwin, *Encyclopedia of Pop, Rock & Soul* (St. Martin's, New York: 1977).

Stetler, Susan, ed., *Almanac of Famous People* (Gale Research, Detroit: 1989).

Stetler, Susan, Ed., *Biography Almanac* (Gale Research, Detroit: 1987).

Stewart, George, *American Given Names* (Oxford U. Press, New York: 1979.)

Thomas, Lowell, *The Vital Spark* (Doubleday, Garden City, NY: 1959).

Tremain, Ruthsen, *Animals Who's Who* (Scribner, New York: 1982).

Van Doren, Charles, ed., *Webster's American Biographies* (Merriam Webster, Springfield, MA: 1974).

Wallace, Irving, *The Intimate Sex Lives of Famous People* (Delacorte, New York: 1981).

Wallace, Irving, David Wallechinsky, *The Book of Lists #2* (William Morrow, New York: 1980).

Wallechinsky, David, Irving Wallace, *The Book of Lists* (Bantam, New York: 1980).

Wallechinsky, David, Irving Wallace, *The People's Almanac #3* (Bantam, New York: 1981).

Withycombe, E.G., *Oxford Dictionary of English Christian Names* (Oxford U. Press, New York: 1977).

Wlaschin, Ken, *Illustrated Encyclopedia of World's Greatest Movie Stars* (Harmony, New York: 1979).

World Book Encyclopedia.

Yonge, Charlotte, M., *History of Christian Names* (Macmillan, London: 1884 — reprint Gale Research, Detroit: 1966).

INDEX OF JOHNS BY NAME*

224

*Note: Italicized numbers refer to illustrations; dates (e.g., JAN 1) refer to Calendar, pp. 192-215.

Index of Other John Information